WHOVIAN DAD

PETE MAY

"Here was a writer called Pete May hailing dear old Alistair Lethbridge-Stewart as 'the man for all invasions. The greatest ever living English chap to fire five rounds rapid at that chap with the wings.' It was all very funny and my wife was at once amused and appalled. For better or worse I appear to have played my part in the creation of a modern-day icon. It is quite a thought."

Nicholas Courtney, aka The Brigadier, from Still Getting Away With It, by Nicholas Courtney and Michael McManus

CONTENTS

ACKNOWLEDGMENTS

Thanks to Bill Williamson, James Brown, Adam Scott and Steve Chamberlain for publishing my features on Doctor Who in this timestream and also to Nicholas Clee for his helpful advice. Gratitude is also due to my fellow Whovians for help and inspiration over the years including Christian Graham, Michael McManus, Mat Coward, Nigel Kendall, Mark Campbell, Doctor Squee, Nick Toms, Nikki Davies, Sharon Brooks, Angharad Beurle-Williams, Martin Woolley, David Goldthorpe, Bob Gilbert and regenerated fans Kevin Beurle and Paul Garrett. And above all to my family, Nicola Baird, Lola May and Nell May for putting up with a man who refuses to hang up his sonic screwdriver.

Pete May, London, August 2014

1. GENESIS OF A WHOVIAN

Growing up with classic Doctor Who... Daleks, Yetis, foaming seaweed, UNIT chaps, Tom Baker, Davros, Davison, Adric's death, Ace's baseball bat and ultimate cancellation.

When did I become a Whovian? I'm pretty sure it's on December 12 1963, at the end of episode one of *The Mutants*, when schoolteacher Barbara Wright is screaming in terror as she is threatened by a disembodied sink plunger. I'm four years and four months old at the time and in short trousers, but my parents seem unaware that this is no normal Saturday teatime TV viewing. And after Barbara's screams comes that pulsating, insistent, otherworldly theme tune. Der... der... der...

The complete Dalek creatures emerge in episode two. I've never seen anything like them. They have thick metal bumpers that glide along the floor of their city. Plus circular bumps on their lower halves, chicken wire wrapped round their waists, a short and deadly death ray alongside their longer arm (which ends with either a sucker or a metallic claw) and spinning heads with one eye on a metal stalk.

When the Daleks kill the Thals, the black and white colours of our TV set are reversed, to terrifying effect in my Essex lounge. But best of all is their rasping mechanical, utterly alien voices, every consonant emphasised. Very soon this child is imitating them: "It will be the end of the Dar-leks..."

It's quite likely that I've seen the first *Doctor Who* story *100,000 BC*, broadcast on Nov 23, where Susan is at school and Barbara and Ian are her teachers before being transported in the Tardis to the Stone Age. But it doesn't have anything like the impact of this.

The Dalek city on the planet Skaro is an eerie place. Mechanical beats throb in the background, Daleks glide over metal floors, electric doors shut with the mysterious whirr of alien machinery. Ron Grainer and his BBC Radiophonic Workshop make up for the cardboard and plastic jungles with some brilliantly inventive sound effects, including, it's said, grating a key on piano wire for the Tardis landings and take-offs.

Many images stay with me for years: that long trek across the mountains to the rear of the Dalek city, with deadly tentacle creatures in the pools. The blonde race of Thals, (whom in later VHS years I discover look uncannily like 1980s New Romantics), the elderly Doctor kneeling under a spotlight being interrogated by the Daleks...

William Hartnell plays the Doctor as a cantankerous old granddad who really shouldn't be fighting alien life forms at his age. He's mysterious and slightly threatening, always irritated with meddling teachers Barbara and Ian, but normally talked round by granddaughter Susan Foreman. Though as the series develops, so my trust in him increases.

Doctor Who becomes regular Saturday evening viewing in our house. The historical episodes are a disappointment, as I always want monsters not boring period drama. But you never know when a story is going to end and a new one might begin featuring the Daleks or some other incredible monsters. Soon, when I'm five, the delicious terror returns in a six-part story *The Dalek Invasion of Earth*. The Daleks are even scarier on Earth. They are attempting to mine down to the planet's core and turn the Earth into a giant spaceship. They have black Daleks now too, and a new catch phrase of "exterminate!"

A few weeks later the Zarbi on *The Web Planet* make a similar terrifying impression on my young mind as my mum is making our tea. Can they really be giant ants? And that landscape of rocks and a black sky encrusted with stars looks just like the pictures in the books I'm reading about the Moon and outer space...

The Chase in the summer of 1965 features more Daleks and briefly another set of robots, the circular Mechanoids. They talk in code and have been holding poor Steven Taylor prisoner for two years.

Now I'm attending primary school it becomes clear to me that my passion is shared by other children. In the playground we impersonate Daleks with our arms outstretched as we re-enact the battles on Mechanus.

Why does *Doctor Who* appeal so much? Is there something in my background that makes me susceptible to science-fiction? There's no nursery school for under-fives as there is today and much of my childhood is spent playing alone. Perhaps this breeds a certain dreaminess and embryonic geekiness. My sister Pam is four years older than me and laughs with my mum as I hide behind the sofa saying that "I'm not scared!' My mum and dad are busy running a dairy farm. We live in the countryside on a council farm tenancy five miles from Brentwood, and my parents don't have much time or inclination for visitors. There's freedom to walk across fields, look at meandering streams in woods, ride a tricycle in the garden and dream of aliens and other world.

And *Doctor Who* just all seems so utterly alien. My world is visits from my Uncle David on Saturdays for afternoon tea and polite conversation over Battenberg cake and fish paste on bread. It's Angel Delight for dessert, cold meat and chips on Mondays and occasional sweets. The most mysterious event is the arrival of the soot-encrusted coalman who plods along the terrace delivering black bags of coal to our shed. But here on TV are terrifying creatures, different planets, death, escape and adventure, and to me and every other kid watching, it is real.

My weekly diet of *Doctor Who* is supplemented by the arrival of a comic called *TV21*. Delivered by the newsagent's boy at increasingly erratic hours each week. I sit by a storage heater, trying to keep warm and wondering when it will arrive... and when it does there are *Doctor Who* cartoon strips and photos of Daleks and pictures from *Thunderbirds* and *Stingray* too.

My uncle David buys me a 45rpm record of The

Daleks, which is the sound recording of the Dalek bits from *The Chase* when the Mechanoids and Daleks are engaged in their fierce battle. Now I can hear their deep voices intoning "I obey!" simply by putting the record on my parents' Radiogram.

The bits where the Daleks use their cutting equipment and travel up lifts are full of tension. I empathise with Steven Taylor's despair at ever escaping his prison in the city above the jungle. There's a lovely emotional bit at the end where Ian says he wants to sit in a pub again and travel on a London bus and end this aimless wandering in time and space. The Doctor gets cross but eventually accedes and it feels like losing old friends as Barbara and Ian return to swinging London.

And then there are the films. My mum takes me to the Brentwood Odeon to see first *Dr Who and the Daleks* in 1965 and then *Daleks — Invasion Earth 2150AD* in 1966. She looks a little bemused by it all as hundreds of children cry "Look! Daleks!" upon their first appearance. The Doctor is played by Peter Cushing with Bernard Cribbins as a policeman who stumbles on to the Tardis and Roberta Tovey playing the Barbara role. But no one minds too much because the Daleks are in vivid Technicolor. Red Daleks, blue Daleks, black Daleks all on a giant screen... and a flying saucer with a rotating top half and Robomen wearing shiny black plastic outfits too.

Back on TV, Vikings, monks and record players seem eerie enough in *The Time Meddler,* while there's an epic dose of Daleks in *The Daleks' Master Plan*. Something completely horrible and terrifying appears at the end of *The Tenth Planet* in October 1966. Under a cloak is the huge form of a silver Cyberman, half robot yet half human, its body regulated by a device on its chest. The Cybermen possess strangely musical but menacing mechanical voices. There's an Arctic base under siege and then the Doctor starts to behave strangely, collapses in the Tardis, and his face starts to change...

I'm starting to read the *Radio Times* for its *Doctor Who* listings and in my parents' *Daily Telegraph* there's a reference to the change. Old William Hartnell is to be replaced by an actor called Patrick Troughton. I'm not sure about this. But the new bloke's all right. In fact he's great. He seems a bit of a clown at first but there's an undercurrent of seriousness behind it all and the Doctor seems genuinely terrified of the dark forces he encounters. And Troughton can certainly run a lot faster than William Hartnell. Oh my giddy aunt!

The arrival of Patrick Troughton doesn't affect my delight at receiving the 1966 *Doctor Who* annual for Christmas, with William Hartnell and the Tardis on the front, accompanied by the Zarbi and Menoptra. My collection of Lego bricks also allows me to make square-shaped Daleks doing battle inside alien cities. And soon will come real toy Daleks...

It's 1967 and suddenly wonderful new monsters seem to appear in every story. Cybermen stalk the transparent dome of *The Moonbase* before floating off into space thanks to the Doctor's strategic use of a gravitron device. A claw in space appears on the Tardis scanner as the Tardis departs from the Moon,

Polly screams and we are into *The Macra Terror*. Even normal-sized crabs in buckets on Southend Pier terrify me after that. Daleks glide around a Victorian house in *The Evil of the Daleks* and order poor, pretty young Victoria not to feed the flying pests.

We're at my grandparents' house in Stoke-on-Trent when *The Tomb of the Cybermen* is broadcast. Here's my granddad, who fought in the first world war, now only able to walk with the aid of a Zimmer frame, filling up his pipe on the arm of his armchair. My grandmother keeps the meat in the pantry because they don't have a fridge. The house is full of dark sideboards and wallpaper turned yellow by smoke; yet on the Bakelite TV screen Cybermen are punching their way through membranes as a vast bank of them emerge from their tomb. My grandfather talks about Stanley Matthews and my dad reads the paper because adults don't watch futuristic rubbish about bug-eyed monsters on children's TV. But to me it's he most incredible thing I've ever seen.

In my primary school playground we imitate the hissing dialogue of *The Ice Warriors*. Occasionally my family venture into London on the underground, but now in *The Web of Fear* something horrible lurks in the tunnels. Yetis with web guns emerge from the darkness, shooting UNIT shoulders and there's nowhere to hide. Then comes foaming seaweed spurting out of ventilator grilles and spawning something evil in *Fury From The Deep*.

Throughout the glory years of Patrick Troughton my biggest fear is of missing an episode of *Doctor*

Who. Luckily my family don't leave the farm for holidays, but my dad does insist on day trips. Sometimes we drive in the Zodiac up to the sights of London like St Paul's Cathedral. But the days out always seem to end unhappily with my dad berating my mum's map reading and the kids crying in the back of the car. On one day trip we're held up for ages in traffic and the agony sinks in of knowing all hope of seeing *Doctor Who* has gone. But then we get home and discover that instead of being on at 5.25 *Doctor Who* is now on an hour later because of the Eurovision Song Contest. Rarely have I felt such unconstrained joy.

I'm nine when the second Ice Warrior story *The Seeds of Death* is screened in 1969, but still absolutely traumatised by that sensation of hiding in a room as an Ice Warrior searches the T-mat base on the Moon. When the Warriors use their ray guns the picture distorts and brave men die. The character of Fewsham is particularly disturbing because he's cracking up and so terrified of the Ice Warriors that he betrays humanity. And many of us might do the same. Then the Patrick Troughton era ends with a long saga called *The War Games* and the revelation that the Doctor is a Time Lord.

In 1970 the Doctor re-emerges in colour and is played as a flamboyant Dandy by Jon Pertwee. He's now confined to Earth and helping UNIT. It's my final year at primary school and *Doctor Who* fans like me take pride in knowing that UNIT stands for United Nations Intelligence Task Force and that its staff consists of Brigadier Alistair Gordon Lethbridge-Stewart, Captain Mike Yates, Sergeant

Benton and a lot of privates who usually get monstered in action. The Brigadier is particularly appealing with his pencil moustache and wry humour, a posh Army type up against it with home counties invasions every few weeks.

It seems scarier now the Doctor is Earthbound and the monsters are viewed in full colour luminous green or brown. Numerous iconic images are captured in my memory. Those plastic mannequins coming alive and breaking out of their shop windows in *Spearhead from Space*, the Silurians lurking in caves, the incessant drilling through the Earth's crust in *Inferno*.

Season eight starts in 1971 and coincides with my first year at secondary school. Quite often I watch *Doctor Who* round at my friend Nick's house, where all shoes have to be removed at the door and slippers donned. But Nick's dad Harold sits down and watches the Doctor with us and seems to really enjoy it. "Look, I bet it's the Master!" he declares. This is a surprise to me, since my own dad wouldn't dream of becoming involved in children's TV. It's not my dad's fault, that's just the way most of his generation acts, but I vow that if I ever have children then one day I'll watch *Doctor Who* with them.

The Master posing as a vicar seems incredibly subversive in *The Dæmons,* though it might explain why I hated the church choir when my parents briefly insisted I join. Long barrows, heat barriers and Brigadier Lethbridge-Stewart ordering five rounds rapid at a gargoyle in a pristine English village create a fantastic, threatening and hugely enjoyable story.

Jon Pertwee is very much a father figure to those around him. He can be irascible but he's also gentle and full of compassion for humans. Pertwee's Doctor realises that people who want to change the future must be very scared indeed in *Day of the Daleks*; and in *Planet of the Daleks* I'm struck by his statement that true bravery is being scared and then going ahead and doing it anyway.

My father has his good qualities, but he's insistent that I must obey him and become a farmer and I'm insistent that I don't like working with cattle. His idea of us working together is to whip me into shape some sergeant major type hollering and that's exactly the way to make me even more determined to follow my own course in life. Pertwee exudes a wisdom that I'd like to see in my home life and perhaps for me and many other children, the Doctor become a surrogate father figure for 25 minutes each Saturday. Though I can't see my dad donning a cape and frilly shirt just yet.

More crazy new monsters arrive from the sea in *The Sea Devils* (though why are they wearing string vests?). The giant maggots emerging out of Welsh mines in *The Green Death* are both surreal and terrifying to my 13-year-old eyes in 1973. I'm also starting to like Jo Grant's boots and tank tops, but there's a very sad goodbye as she marries Dr Cliff Jones and leaves a rueful Doctor at the end. Though thankfully her replacement Sarah Jane Smith is very capable of tackling Sontarans in medieval castles

Jon Pertwee departs at the end of season 11 and Tom Baker arrives as the latest Doctor in December

1974. An article in my parents' *Daily Telegraph* reveals that he was working on a building site when he got the part. Baker is goggle-eyed and weird, very alien and simply superb as a Time Lord. *Genesis of the Daleks* has me entranced. The shrunken figure of Davros is a superb creation. At the end of the six-parter we're left with a Dalek eye stalk smack in the middle of the TV screen that stands just by my fireplace and Welsh dresser in my house. It's telling us that the Daleks might be entombed but when the time is right they will take their place as the supreme beings in the universe.

There's less of UNIT, the show is more like a Hammer horror movie now. Cybermen skulk around in caves, Zygons lurk under Loch Ness, Martian mummies come alive, I'm particularly excited when the decaying body under a black robe in *The Deadly Assassin* is revealed to be the Master, returning for the first time since the Pertwee years.

Of course, there are rival attractions when I become a proper teenager. My love of football takes me to West Ham games on some Saturdays and there is pressure to shop for wide-collared flowery shirts at Mr Byrite in Romford on Saturday afternoons and sometimes the bus is late home. If I can ever impress girls it surely won't be through talking about *Doctor Who*. Smoking Players' No 6, drinking Watney's Party Seven and getting amorous at Mountnessing Village Hall discos appears to be the approach of my more laddish peers.

By the time I'm in the sixth form at school I know that *Doctor Who* is a bit silly, but everyone still regards it with almost universal affection. Tom

Baker and his scarf seamlessly fit into our school culture of *Monty Python's Flying Circus*, *the Goodies*, Rod Stewart and the Faces, Bryan Ferry, Elton John, Mott the Hoople, *Match of the Day* and *the Old Grey Whistle Test*.

Tom Baker is there throughout my university years too. It becomes a Saturday afternoon ritual to watch Tom in the County College TV room and to laugh at the giant prawn that is the virus in *The Invisible Enemy* and what appears to be a monstrous phallus in *The Creature From The Pit*. But everyone also enjoys Tom's over-the-top performance. Baker is joined by Lalla Ward as Romana, who's a Lady in real life according to the *Daily Mirror* in the Junior Common Room. And there are huge cheers in the college TV room when John Cleese makes a cameo appearance at the end of *City of Death*, as *Who* and *Python* and *Fawlty Towers* merge for one total sofa meltdown student moment.

Back at home in the Christmas vacation of 1979 there's more *Who* watching to be done with my nine-year-old younger sister Caroline, ten years my junior. We settle down to watch *The Horns of Nimon*. She's very scared of the Nimon and its booming voice. I'm reminded of my own childhood tremors, while on a more adult level enjoying the exuberant overacting of Graham Crowden as Soldeed.

When Baker leaves and is replaced by Peter Davison in January 1982 the Doctor's wanderings in time and space are coinciding with my own wanderings around mostly terrible flatshares in

London. Davison doesn't seem right; to me he's still Tristan in *All Creatures Great and Small,* and evokes memories of Sunday nights at my mum and dad's and hands up cow's bottoms. He's too young and lacks the required gravitas. *Doctor Who* also changes times, to an unfamiliar midweek slot. Which in some ways makes my watching easier, but still seems to be fundamentally wrong when everyone knows *Doctor Who* should be on a Saturday.

Still, I'm really impressed by *Earthshock* in early 1982 as I watch in a rented room in Turnpike Lane. The way the Cyber Leader says "Excellent!" is, well, excellent. The denouement explains the mystery of how the dinosaurs were wiped out — it wasn't an asteroid, but a nuclear explosion caused by the Cybermen's craft crash landing into the Earth. This was all thanks to the sacrifice of companion Adric. Although Adric is spotty and a bit annoying, his death is shocking because companions just don't die. The silent credits at the end are striking and a great *Who* moment.

When *The Five Doctors* celebrates the show's 20th anniversary in 1983 I'm unhappily ensconced with some wannabe Sloane Rangers in Fulham Road. But I enjoy seeing Cybermen zapped by the Rassilon robot and the Doctors grapple with another chess-set style puzzle to enter a forbidden city.

Other episodes are up and down. *Warriors of the Deep* trashes all my wonderful memories of *Sea Devils, Resurrection of the Daleks* contains Bob (Rodney Bewes) from *Whatever Happened to The Likely Lads* and is filmed at the derelict Shad

Thames by London Bridge, which I've recently visited. *Planet of Fire* is poor but the following week's *The Caves of Androzani* is superbly directed by Graeme Harper and realistic and hard-hitting. How do they manage to vary the quality so much?

My interest wanes almost completely when Colin Baker is appointed as the next Doctor in March 1984. He was ok in *The Brothers* as Paul Merroney, but now he's playing the Doctor as a bit of a weirdo who tries to strangle Peri and is dressed in some sort of ridiculous multi-coloured patchwork outfit that looks it was rejected as way to outlandish for the Finnish contestants in the Eurovision Song Contest. The show is veering towards pantomime, although Peri's cleavage impresses my mate John as we occasionally watch in yet another shared gaff in Camberwell. The human head encased in a transparent Dalek in *Revelation off the Daleks* is impressive.

Doctor Who is cancelled for a season in 1985, sparking a terrible *Doctor In Distress* single, penned by uber fan and continuity adviser Ian Levine. It features Colin Baker singing and members of Dollar and Bucks Fizz in an inglorious Live Aid pastiche. The BBC relents and *Doctor Who* returns in the autumn of 1986 with the 14-episode *The Trial of a Time Lord,* which becomes a meandering trial of the visual senses. Appointing Bonnie Langford as a companion is surely the act of someone trying to destroy the show, while casting Brian Blessed as King Yrcanos only adds to the end-of-pier atmosphere.

When Baker is ignominiously sacked and

replaced by Sylvester McCoy in 1987 the show initially fails to improve. So what keeps me with *Doctor Who*? By this stage I've become a freelance journalist and I'm staring to appreciate the cultural impact Doctor Who has had. My collection of VHS videos is growing too. Suddenly great chunks of my childhood re-emerge. *The Seeds of Death* reveals the Ice Warriors to be almost as scary as in my memory, although some idiot has edited out all the cliffhangers. *The Day of the Daleks* reminds me of Jon Pertwee's charm while *The Robots of Death* shows Tom Baker at his peak. They convince me that all *Doctor Who* needs is to have a man of gravitas playing the Doctor. Under producer John Nathan-Turner there are way too many celebrity cameos and silly sparkly costumes. No way should *Doctor Who* ever be played for laughs. It has to be played seriously or it's nothing.

A black TV and black VHS video recorder from Currys add a homely touch to my latest flat, a short-life housing association flat in an asbestos-ridden council tower block in Westbourne Park. *Doctor Who* returns in October 1988 and I record all four episodes of *Remembrance of the Daleks* on one VHS tape. And it's really very good. Gone is the kitsch. A Dalek levitates up stairs at the end of part one, answering an age-old quandary about how the Daleks planned to dominate the universe without being able to climb stairs.

The Daleks have proper menacing voices again, the support players are excellent and it's in a convincing 1963 setting. Ace, played by Sophie Aldred, is a companion who doesn't scream and inspires the enduring admiration of a partnerless man in W9 as she whacks Daleks with a baseball bat. Best of all, the Imperial Daleks and renegade Daleks fight each in a galactic version of the Militant Tendency versus the SWP, while the Emperor Dalek is revealed to have a ranting Davros beneath its domed head.

I record all the remaining episodes, including a Maggie Thatcher figure and Liquorice Allsorts monster in *The Happiness Patrol* and scary clowns in *The Greatest Show In The Galaxy*. In 1989 *The Curse of Fenric* features an outstanding performance from Nicholas Parsons, of all people, as a vicar losing his faith. The story is full of atmosphere and has something evocative that hasn't been seen in *Doctor Who* for years. *Survival* shows promise too, but then Sylvester and Sophie walk off into a purple sky at the end and that's it. Series 26 finishes on December 6 1989 and there's no word of any more *Doctor Who* from Michael Grade and the BBC.

So this is it. The Doctor has been with me for nearly all my 29 years of life and now he's gone. Not even the imminent VHS video release of *The Daleks* can compensate for this. Will there ever be a series 27? Or has the Doctor finally been exterminated?

2. THE WILDERNESS YEARS

Keeping the faith in the dark days of the 1990s... Behind the Sofa at MOMI, Dæmons and Jon Pertwee in Wiltshire, and four Doctors in Hammersmith.

Season 26 of *Doctor Who* has finished and the programme is now lost in time and space. The BBC's controller Michael Grade is an enemy of the Doctor and there seems little chance of it ever returning — even if the BBC will never officially admit that it has been axed, possibly because it is under the control of the Master.

Just as I've returned to the Doctor it has ended. It seems an act of incredible stupidity by the BBC. Every video release of *Doctor Who* is still going in at the top of the charts. It has run from 1963 to 1989. My own VHS collection is burgeoning thanks to regular trips to the Virgin Megastore on Oxford Street: *Day of The Daleks*, *The Talons of Weng Chiang*, *Spearhead from Space*... and I have a nice wooden rack, also from the Virgin Megastore, on which I can store my videos in chronological order. Though sometimes I rearrange them in alphabetical order just for a change.

There's still an army of fanatical fans devoted to the programme. Yes, there have been problems with stupid cameo appearances, sparkly costumes and show being played as a pantomime in the later years. But *Remembrance of the Daleks* and sections of *The Curse of Fenric* showed how good it could still be. Imagine what might happen if the BBC put some love and money into it!

The art of making good *Doctor Who* is to take it seriously, I declare over a pint or four with my old school friend Paul Garrett as we reminisce about Brigadier Lethbridge-Stewart and chaps with wings in early 1990. Paul argues that there had to be no more running down corridors and calling one room 'the citadel' and making it represent a whole race. But we agree that it needs an actor of gravitas to take over the role, someone like Anthony Hopkins, allied with much better production values and a Saturday night show rather than up against *Coronation Street* in midweek.

Having made it into the world of journalism I make it my duty to slip the Doctor into articles wherever I can. A piece for the Red Wedge magazine *Well Red* suggests an uncanny prediction of Thatcherite economic policy in my new video of *Day of the Daleks*. The Daleks tell the Controller that it doesn't matter if weak workers die as inefficient workers slow down production. I suggest that Douglas Hurd is a Dalek, Thatcher is Davros, Geoffrey Howe is a Mechanoid, Norman Tebbit an ice Warrior and that hairy Michael Heseltine might be a Yeti. Strangely, my withering political satire appears to partially work, as Margaret Thatcher finally resigns as Prime Minster in November 1990.

The new satellite TV networks know a dedicated audience that is bigger on the inside and are still giving *Doctor Who* airtime. BskyB's Galaxy Channel runs a whole *Doctor Who* weekend in September 1990 and I'm soon sending videos over to my friend Steve's sister Hannah, who is a subscriber, asking her to tape the Yeti rarities.

Midweek, a free magazine for London commuters, publishes my full-page preview of the weekend under the headline 'The Exterminator'. Those chunky BBC videos, with their green labels and thick plastic, that today feel a heavy as bricks, are proving very useful.

My piece recounts the plot of *The Daleks*, Hartnell's winning mix of irascibility and mysteriousness, and the lure of the Daleks: "Accentuated by the black and white filming the scenes in the Daleks' metallic city are genuinely eerie, all sliding doors and the hum of alien machinery. The world's first glimpse of a Dalek is unforgettable. Barbara cowers in terror as a disembodied sink plungers moves towards her…" It also takes the Mickey out of the Thals, suggesting they looked "like a race of Scandinavians wearing Abba's discarded shoulder pads."

It mentions some of the very adult themes of Terry Nation's story; how the Daleks are the result of a massive nuclear war that destroyed people not buildings and now need radiation to live; the Hitler parallels of these 'superior beings' in *The Dalek Invasion of Earth*; and bringing it into the 1990s my piece suggests that the Daleks' plan to control the environment was "an uncanny philosophy of the folly that lead to today's Green movement."

My memories are still vivid of my Westbourne Park flat and my friend Annie's Italian boyfriend laughing hysterically at the camp Robomen as we played the Peter Cushing film *Daleks — Invasion*

Earth 2150AD. "The best thing about the film is the Robomen," I write, "humans robotised by the Daleks who wander the streets clad in shiny black PVC, crash helmets and goggles, carrying whips and looking as if they're all fetishists off to a perverts' ball."

The article also looks forward to the Yeti programme and remarks what a tragedy it is that only one episode of *The Web of Fear* remains, explaining how the BBC had wiped numerous Troughton and Hartnell episodes and suggesting that whoever committed this act of vandalism should be exterminated.

My fellow journalist 'Cyber' Mat Coward is writing columns for *Midweek* and *New Statesman*, and as we are both periodically working for the same magazines, we soon establish a Whovian rapport. Mat enjoys the splits between the Doctor Who Appreciation Society (DWAS) and *Doctor Who Bulletin* and how it mirrors those on the left: the fact that you can attack someone for having a fundamentally unsound line on the Pertwee era makes us both chuckle.

DWAS is the largest fan group with about 1500 members, but just as there was a split between Davros' Imperial Daleks and the Renegade Daleks in *Remembrance of the Daleks*, so DWAS, the only group officially recognised by the BBC is fighting off Whovian splinter groups. Younger fans complain of a 'DWAS clique'. In 1990 the more militant *Doctor Who Bulletin* magazine mounts a phone-in to the BBC demanding a series 27, a move that DWAS refuses to support. DWAS mounts another campaign though, where fans send the BBC cheques for £5 payable to *Doctor Who* to put towards the cost of a new series. It claims that £7500 has been sent to the BBC in this way. Meanwhile, the DWAS magazine *Celestial Toyroom* notes that a number of societies have affiliated with the Midlands-based Whonatics.

Mat suggests that the Cybermen are like the Socialist Workers Party (he's thinking of David Banks' Cyber Leader here) with their cold ruthless logic and intellectual posturing on the inevitability of the collapse of the Doctor, while the Daleks are much more like the Militant Tendency. He suggests that the "Do not deviate, do not deviate, let no opposition halt you!" line in *Destiny of the Daleks* is a direct reference to Militant leader Peter Taafe. Trotskyists are indeed very worried about deviation from socialist policies and betrayal of the working class policies.

Perhaps Cyber Mat is on to something. Alan Bleasdale includes a *Doctor Who* convention in *GBH*, his 1991 series about a socialist council leader Michael Murray. As Murray, about to sleep with Barbara, desperately searches for condoms in the luxury hotel, Daleks in the corridor chant "Fornicate! Fornicate!"

The Museum of the Moving Image in London mounts its *Behind the Sofa* exhibition in June 1991, a show devoted exclusively to *Doctor Who*. I've already nabbed a brilliant MOMI t-shirt that arrives at *Time Out*, where I'm doing subbing shifts. It spells out the theme tune on its chest: "Dumba-de-dum Dumba-de-dum Dumba-de-dum diddleydum… Wah-aaaaaaaah!"

Commissioned to write a piece on the exhibition for *Midweek*, I attend the Behind the Sofa launch party with Nikki Bowden the art editor on *Ms London*, a Kiwi Whovian who is eventually set to work for the BBC's *Doctor Who Adventures* magazine.

"Greetings to the Panopticon! I am the keeper of the Matrix…" announces an actor dressed as a Time Lord. The Panopticon is the main room of the Capitol on Gallifrey and its six sides have statues of the six founders of Time Lord society. We walk past TV monitors playing excerpts from classic *Who*.

"I remember those giant maggots! 1974 Saturday nights, fish and chips on the sheepskin rug!" declares Nikki in a stream of Whovian consciousness. Clearly the programme had been as big an influence in New Zealand as it had here.

"The attack of the giant condoms…" continues Nikki "They look just like weta bugs"(these are the world's largest bugs from Kiwiland).

We find a hands-on Dalek that you can get inside, and waggle its sink plunger and chant "Exterminate!" through a voice modifier.

"It's a boiler suit sprayed silver!" someone says of the Cyberman costume in front of us. There's an impressive array of costumes: Ice Warriors in shades, Yetis, Silurians, Sea Devils, Vervoids, Plasmatrons, Tetraps. Garm, Axons and numerous other creatures the colour of a festering vindaloo.

We loiter by the display case of *Doctor Who* memorabilia. Here we find numerous model Daleks from the 1960s, *Who* jigsaws, *Doctor Who* milk chocolate, K9 models and much more.

I ask David Howe, the owner of the collection, about his *Doctor Who* underpants. "I got these from Woolworths in 1978," he tells me proudly. Howe, eventually to become a personal hero of mine for co-writing *Doctor Who: The Television Companion*, says he has left DWAS and is now producing his own magazine *The Frame*, available from "FP' as he terms Forbidden Planet.

There's a lot of drinking of white wine and Becks beer going on in the main party area and we find Ace, aka Sophie Aldred, surrounded by foreign TV crews. Eventually I manage to grab a few words for *Midweek*. "I hid behind the cushion rather than the sofa," she says of growing up in the Pertwee era and adds that meeting Pertwee at a convention made her feel like a child again.

Aldred talks about appearing in the children's series *Melvin and Maureen's Musicogrammes* and says she's hopeful of working with "Sylv" again on *Doctor Who,* because it was great fun.

Suddenly a voice cries "Sophie!" She answers "Nick!" And it's the Brigadier Nicholas Courtney embracing the former companion in actorly fashion before whisking her off to other parts of MOMI.

My pal Nikki has had a Becks or two and is chatting to a Time Lord. "Welcome carbon based bipeds. Why is it necessary to drink this substance called alcohol? This is not necessary on the planet Gallifrey," says the chap with the funny neck display.

"Don't you get hot in that costume?" asks Nikki.

"I should say so, I can't even raise my arm in this bloody thing," he exclaims slipping out of character and revealing that he's one of MOMI's in-house actors. "I think it went downhill after Tom Baker left myself. They can't get the scriptwriters anymore. Hey, he's got a drink – how did he get a drink?"

"Look that Cyberman's throwing up!' laughs Nikki as we gaze at a clip from The Five Doctors.

A Dalek-shaped cake is being cut by Nick Courtney, Bonnie Langford, Carole Anne Ford (the Doctor's granddaughter!) and Sophie Aldred. Whonatics, hacks, actors and hot Time Lords materialise by the free drinks table and demand the making of series 27 while the Ron Grainer theme plays all around MOMI. I slip out and walk home across Hungerford Bridge to my new short-life gaff in Victoria, a happy Whovian.

For a time my romantic life also seems to be intertwined with *Doctor Who*. For six months I date Sue, a probation officer living in Brixton who has two daughters. Only she still shares a house she's bought with her ex-boyfriend Kevin, a real-life scientist who designs space probes to Jupiter. This is a complicated arrangement until Kevin and I discover that Kevin is a Whovian. We bond over *The Web Planet*, as Kevin remarks, "I see the Menoptra are still having a hard time…" While Sue's elder daughter, eight-year-old Angharad, is won over by my bringing over my VHS tape of *The Curse of Fenric*.

A few months later after my relationship with Sue ends (though let's credit her for having the courage to date serial Whovians) I become involved with Octavia, a poet and arts administrator, who eventually rings up to tell me there's something missing from our relationship, just when I'm playing my new video of *Genesis of the Daleks* for the first time.

"I'm just not ready to give or receive, I'm having doubts… are you playing *Doctor Who*?" she asks, having overheard the theme. I have to admit that I am. It wouldn't be so bad if she'd phoned at a different moment. But during *Genesis of the Daleks*? She dumps me for a man from a TV company just before the really good bit where the Dalek tells Davros that pity is not registered in its vocabulary banks and for several months (well, maybe weeks) I'm too upset to watch the best ever *Doctor Who*, as voted by readers of *Doctor Who Magazine*.

For five months in 1992 I travel round Australia and New Zealand, wondering where my life is going. But the Doctor doesn't desert me. I'm in a hotel room in Broome and there's Tom Baker in *The Invisible Enemy*. *Doctor Who* is being replayed weekly on Australian TV and now a giant prawn wants to make contact with the Swarm.

Upon my return to England references to the Doctor continue to permeate my journalism. My editors must be very tolerant. A *Midweek* feature on my new home at Elephant and Castle suggests that it would be no surprise to see a Sontaran emerge from the strange cuboid building that looks like a crashed spaceship on the Elephant and Castle roundabout.

At *Time Out* the weekly Sidelines news and gossip column falls into my hands. It's a chance to promote all things Whovian. Better still, free things start turning up at the office. Who videos, spin-off books, t-shirts, records. Copies of *Doctor Who Bulletin* (later *DWB* and the *Dreamwatch*) also turn up at *Time Out*, with reviews of classics like *The Caves of Androzani* and plenty of attacks on anyone to do with 1980s *Doctor Who* and in particular producer John Nathan Turner.

In May 1993 Sidelines covers the launch of the 30th anniversary year at the futuristic Arc building in Hammersmith. Doctors Jon Pertwee, Peter Davison, Colin Baker and Sylvester McCoy are all in attendance, though Tom Baker is away filming *Medics*. This is the first time I've ever been in the same room as four Doctors posing with a black Dalek and *Time Out's* man feels happier than a Cyberman in a cargo hold.

I ask Sylvester McCoy for news on the series returning and he quips, "I'd be the last to know!" There follows a conversation with Nicholas Courtney who repeats the "chap with the wings" line for me, as we discuss his biography *Five Rounds Rapid*. Standing on the fringes of a Sky news crew I hear Jon Pertwee agree that *Who* fans have been treated shabbily.

The highlight of the 30th anniversary bash is when the four Doctors turn on BBC Home Entertainment's Tony Greenwood, after he admits that the Corporation have made £10 million from *Doctor Who* videos. Greenwood tells the Doctors that, "Alan Yentob has said the door is not closed."

To which Jon Pertwee replies, wittily and poignantly: "Can you hurry up, because the door's closing on me anytime now!"

A projected £750,000 30th anniversary show is killed by the BBC's internal politics, though 1993 does see *Doctor Who* back on the cover of *Radio Times* with the headline "Look Who's Back." A documentary show, *Doctor Who: 30 Years in the Tardis* is aired on BBC 2, while Children in Need has *Dimensions in Time* — a rather embarrassing skit featuring cameos by various Doctors and Kate O'Mara as the Rani, all becoming so dispirited that they have to nip into the Queen Vic on the *EastEnders* set for five rounds rapid. It's good to see old faces such as Sarah Jane, Peri, the Brigadier, Mike Yates, Romana and Victoria, but really the last thing we need is another pantomime.

At the end of the year in *Time Out's* Old Ma Sidelines Almanac I predict: "Steven Spielberg's film version of *Doctor Who* is a massive success both here and in the States. The BBC says the show has no future. The Daleks are so outraged that they invade Earth and install John Birt as their puppet leader. Dennis Potter leads the Earthling resistance."

The end of 1993 sees more success on my own companion front though. At the *New Statesman* I meet my eventual wife Nicola, who, like most women in the 1990s, is not a Whovian. But Nicola comes from a much posher family than my own and I soon discover that she is a distant relative of Lalla Ward, who as we all know played Romana alongside Tom Baker. Here is a woman who is related to Whovian royalty. Her grandmother has even met Tom Baker and Ward's current husband Richard Dawkins. Any sort of *Doctor Who* connection has to be a good sign for the future.

Despite being in her thirties Nicola cowers behind the sofa if Doctor Who comes on my video. So my *Who* fests have to be solitary affairs when she's out of the house. Other men have secret stashes of erotic 'art' films on VHS, but I just have Hartnell to McCoy-era *Who*.

We move in to Nicola's flat in Highbury, where she holds literary salons, with a different person presenting a topic each month. My gathering involves showing 12 of our friends the full video of *The Dæmons*. The Islingtonites find Jon Pertwee's attitude to Jo a little sexist and patronising (and he was particularly grumpy in that episode), but everyone enjoys the heat barrier around Devil's End, the Reverend Magister and Bok, that chap with the wings.

Soon I'm reviewing all the *Doctor Who* video releases for *Time Out*. Not 'only do you get free videos off the BBC, *Time Out* pays me £25 per review. Yes. I'm being paid to watch *Doctor Who*. Nicola's earnest green friends can't quite believe it.

If I'm lucky I get sent the finished BBC video wrapped in cellophane. Otherwise it's a press tape in a white sleeve with a time counter imprinted across the bottom of the picture. Every glimpse of that phallic monster in *The Creature From The Pit* has a seconds, minutes and hours counter whirring round its nether regions. I can create my own video library by taking the Doctor Who video covers sent out to the art department, inserting them into blank video cases and adding the time-coded pre-release cassettes.

Each new video is taken home and played with fevered anticipation. Some episodes I have forgotten, others I suddenly remember after a time-lapse of 25-odd years. Some disappoint, others are better then anticipated. *The Green Death* has all the elements that make *Doctor Who* great — the Doctor fighting a dodgy giant fly, Welsh miners saying 'boyo' a lot, Pertwee in drag, a mad computer, a mention of Nietzsche to baffle the seven-year-olds, UNIT's three-man army being baffled by killer condoms and the Brigadier firing at a dratted caterpillar. Professor Cliff Jones in the Nuthutch (a community that's rather like the Newbury Bypass protestors) reminds me of the *Guardian's* George Monbiot, whom we met when Nicola was living in Oxford. Proof that *Doctor Who* was always prescient.

Many new delights are discovered: William Hartnell going to a disco and robots made of cardboard boxes in *The War Machines*; the crew of a slave-starliner in *Warrior's Gate* eating their lunches out of Tupperware containers; Professor Keller's machine sucking the evil out of criminals' brains in *The Mind Of Evil*; Davros going all new age as the 'great healer' in *Revelation of the Daleks*; and a bashful Cyberman insisting that the Earth woman Peri must have warmer clothing in *Attack of the Cybermen*.

Doctor Who Magazine is a particular delight. While compiling my *Time Out* columns I regularly ring its editor Gary Gillet, hopeful for news of season 27. There are always plenty of rumours, and he is a good source of Whovian gossip. It's astonishing how the magazine keeps going long after *Doctor Who* has left our screens. Fans like me read it and are reassured that they are not alone.

During those long wilderness years I can read in *Doctor Who Magazine* a list of ten moments that make *Doctor Who* the greatest programme ever, six pages on the making of *Genesis of the Daleks,* news that Tom Baker is making some adverts in New Zealand with the Tardis, a Q&A session with Barry Letts, seven pages on missing Troughton episode *Fury From The Deep,* the readers poll of the greatest *Doctor Who* stories of all time (*The Twin Dilemma* comes bottom at number 169) and even a two-page review of *The Power of Kroll* video release.

A series of *New Doctor Who Adventures* novels from Virgin helps keep the Doctor alive. I review fan-produced videos such as *Downtime*, featuring the Brigadier and Victoria among others, being pursued by the Great Intelligence in the grounds of the University of East Anglia.

Who pops up in the most unexpected places. Nicola had worked for two years with Voluntary Service Overseas in the Solomon Islands. We visit the Solomon Islands for a month in 1995, and a drop loo above hundreds of coconut crabs on Bellona brings back terrible memories of menacing claws in the Troughton-era story *The Macra Terror*.

Jon Pertwee's last public appearance is at The Dæmons Reunion Weekend at Aldbourne in

Wiltshire on April 29 1996. Fellow Whovian Kevin Beurle, the ex-boyfriend of Sue in Brixton, drives myself, his daughter Angharad and her sister Bethan down the M4 to Aldbourne.

Kevin is a bit of a Doctor-type scientist himself, plumbing his house "by following first principles" and able to design space satellites and probes to the outer reaches of the solar system.

It's an unusually hot April weekend and the lovely English village is full of bird song and Whovians relaxing in the sunshine. Riders trot through the village passing men in Tom Baker scarves. Bucolic life meets monsters from outer space.

We eat baked potatoes for lunch in the village teashop and chat to two twins from south Wales dressed in Colin Baker and Peter Davison Doctor costumes. That's the church that some viewers thought was really blown up. You almost expect the Reverend Magister to appear from behind a gravestone at any moment. And now we are outside the walls where the Brigadier wanted Jenkins to fire five round rapid at that chap with the wings.

There's time for a pint of real ale in the village pub the Blue Boar, where someone has had the splendid idea of putting up a sign on the pub for the Cloven Hoof, the pub in The Dæmons. Opposite the pub is the very village green where Jon Pertwee was molested by Magister's manic Morris men, brandishing sticks and threatening him with bells, ribbons and dodgy sideburns.

The *Dæmons* has always been one of my favourite ever *Doctor Who* stories with its tales of spaceships found in long barrows, village pubs, Devil-worshipping in the crypt and bicycling white witches. The familiar is always much more frightening.

The event is held on a large field behind the church. *Who* conventions are pleasingly amateur in the 1990s. No laminated badges, just stages made of straw bales, plastic chairs and a white marquee on grass.

Outside the tent there's a Dalek (is it better to have them exterminating outside the tent or inside the tent exterminating out?) with someone inside it operating a voice modulator and small children posing for photos. We take pictures of ourselves with a slightly tatty-looking Ice Warrior and a multi-tentacled Axon. Though modern children prove too much for some of the invaders. An Ice Warrior's arm falls off at one point and then the Dalek's head come off and has to be re-attached with a non-sonic screwdriver.

Jon Pertwee and the UNIT family of Nicholas Courtney, Richard Franklin and John Levene plus Damaris Hayman (the wonderful white witch Miss Hawthorne), Barry Letts and Terrence Dicks, both legends from the Pertwee era, pose by a Dalek as photographers in Chinos and t-shirts snap away. The white-haired Pertwee is wearing a maroon velvet jacket and enjoying the attention, joking with the snappers.

Later there's a huge but orderly queue for signings as the Doctor and his UNIT chaps Yates and Benton sit at a table on the green. Then it's on to the events in the marquee. There's a touching moment early on as Jon Pertwee stands at the entrance of the tent and apologises for having to leave. "I just wanted to say goodbye. I've got to do another job on my musical show. Thank you very much for coming we really do appreciate it." The applause is genuinely warm and unknown to us it is the last time we will see him on the convention circuit.

A series of interviews follow in the overheating marquee. Master of ceremonies is John Levene, no longer Sergeant Benton but now a smooth-talking be-suited salesman living in America, cracking groan-inducing jokes and compering the event.

Nick Courtney is on the stage with a pint of beer in hand, carrying on from where he left off drinking in the Cloven Hoof in 1971, 25 years earlier. He's asked why Jo fancied Yates and not Benton and he suspects it's because rank has its privileges. Courtney reveals he's been to Dalek creator Terry Nation's house in America, and that it has a Dalek standing outside it. Terrence Dicks is also questioned and says at the time of filming he regarded his stay in Aldbourne as "a mild holiday" where he could get ahead on the next show.

As evening falls fireworks are set off over Devil's End. We gaze upwards at the real Venus and Mars as well as the Moon, which is probably being invaded by Cybermen and Ice Warriors as I drink my real ale. I leave Aldbourne with a souvenir Dæmons mug in my hand, some fine pictures of Jon Pertwee and plenty of great memories. *Doctor Who* has never seemed so English, so brilliant and such a loss to the TV cosmos.

Jon Pertwee dies in the United States (or should that be regenerates?) at the age of 76 on May 20 1996. Nigel at *Time Out* recommends me as the magazine's resident Whovian and I find myself on some new-fangled satellite TV channel off Oxford Street providing soundbites. My short interview with the news anchor has me mentioning the Dæmons Reunion and saying that wherever Jon Pertwee now is I hope he has his sonic screwdriver with him.

A week after Pertwee's death some new and much anticipated *Doctor Who* finally arrives. For a year or so I'd been printing rumours in *Time Out* of a projected *Doctor Who* TV film made in the US by 20th Century Fox in a co-production with BBC Enterprises. At one point Eric Idle was rumoured to have been up for the lead role. But now we learn it's Paul McGann as the Doctor —this is very encouraging as he was superb in both the cult film *Withnail and I* and the TV series *The Monocled Mutineer*. The fact it's being made in America is of course a cause for concern, but it's due on British screens on May 27.

In June 1995 I use my London Spy column in *Midweek* to rant against the BBC selling pewter Daleks at £73.50 while ignoring the demand for a British-made series of *Doctor Who*. My column asks: "Can you imagine the US TV and film industry suddenly saying they're tired of old concepts like *Star Trek* and *Batman* and selling them to Britain?"

Still, I watch in some excitement at our shared flat in Highbury as McGann's Doctor arrives in San

Francisco. The first half an hour or so is excellent. Sylvester McCoy appears like an old friend, drinking tea on the Tardis. His regeneration into McGann is certainly memorable. The Tardis crash lands in San Francisco in 1999 and the Doctor is shot. The scenes in the morgue owe a lot to the resurrection of Christ and McGann looks perfect as the new Doctor with his air of alien vulnerability and a costume that is stylish and different but not stupidly outrageous. No question marks anywhere, thank goodness. And executive producer Philip Segal includes some nice nods to the series' past, such as a glimpse of Tom Baker's scarf and the new Doctor's love of jelly babies.

Yet somehow it doesn't seem right after McGann's regeneration. *Doctor Who* has been Americanised in Matthew Jacobs' script in the hope of kickstarting a new US-based series. There are lots of vehicles and chases, with ambulances, bikes and cars. It's all action and not enough thought.

Eric Roberts as the Master is wearing shades and looks like Arnold Schwarzenegger in *The Terminator* and unforgivably, the Doctor has a snog (twice!) with the rather good Grace Holloway, played by Daphne Ashbrook. Jon Pertwee wouldn't have done that... And it's too late to suggest that the Doctor is half human, as this new story does.

The Master tries to steal the Doctor's regenerations through opening up the Eye of Harmony (which was meant to be on Gallifrey according to classic *Who* lore in *The Deadly Assassin*). There's a countdown to the new millennium and the Master ends up falling into the

Eye himself.

It's not bad and McGann is the right actor for the Doctor, but it suffers from a lack of monsters and the fact that it's not made by the BBC in England. McGann shows enough promise for there to be some hope of a new series, but it never materialises. So that's it, a half-decent, but still botched opportunity that looks unlikely to be repeated. *Doctor Who* will probably never return and all we can do is continue to enjoy on video the 696 episodes from the classic series of 1963-1989, that is apart from the ones wiped by BBC Robomen in the 1960s.

But still my personal campaign of restoring the Doctor to the public consciousness carries on. A new lads' magazine called *Loaded* had appeared in 1994, edited by James Brown, covering all the important things in life, such as TV, biscuits, beer, football and women. Its nostalgia for bygone TV programmes makes it a perfect place to push Whovian ideas.

James Brown is immediately enthusiastic about having "The Brigadier off *Doctor Who*" in the Greatest Living Englishmen column. This allows me to watch all the old Jon Pertwee UNIT videos and tell Nicola it's work. My tribute appears in November 1996 and there it is, a picture of Nicholas Courtney as the magnificently mustached Brigadier, in what is now a hugely popular magazine selling half a million copies.

The article details how Courtney played the role with just the right mix of bombast and irony: "He deserves our recognition for his strikingly British reserve in the face of numerous alien invasions by man-eating plastic chairs, Dæmons, dinosaurs, Cybermen, robot Loch Ness monsters, Zygons and giant green maggots on Welsh hillsides."

It praises his skill at solving logistical problems such as how to hold a world peace conference when Daleks and Ogrons are invading the front lawn, and claims that with all the strain of having to deal with the PM and bureaucrats in Geneva it's understandable if he makes the odd error such as mistaking an anti-matter planet for a beach in Cromer, Norfolk. Though in his off-duty moments there is some suggested bedroom action with Doris in Brighton when he visits a clairvoyant in *Planet of the Spiders*.

I write: "The Brig had none of the Doctor's namby-pamby compassion for alien races. Blighters who didn't even go to public school coming over here to invade the Earth —'Let 'em have it Sergeant Benton!' He blew up complete underground stations in *The Web of Fear* and *Invasion of the Dinosaurs*. CHECK Much to the Doctor's disgust he blew up an entire race of Silurians..." Though a little collateral damage is always likely when facing so many invasions of home counties quarries.

That *Loaded* tribute concludes: "Brigadier Alistair Gordon Lethbridge-Stewart. He was the man for all invasions. The greatest living Englishman ever to fire five rounds rapid at that chap with the wings."

In May 1997 *Loaded* publishes another of my Greatest Living Englishmen columns on Tom Baker, compete with a picture of Tom and a speech bubble saying "Hello old thing!"

"Baker did what any sensible Time Lord would do when confronted by weekly armies of aliens bent on universal domination. He took the piss out of them," I write, before quoting many of his best lines.

The piece mentions the Doctor coming over all *Guardian* reader when he can't decide whether to prevent the Daleks ever existing in *Genesis of the Daleks* and praised his costume and jelly babies. "It takes a top Time Lord to play with a yo-yo while he's get a Cyberman bomb strapped to his back... Tom Baker you made the Doctor the greatest living Gallifreyan geezer in the Universe."

Alongside a Ray Winstone interview and Sara Cox in a glamour shoot, the December issue of *Loaded* talks to David Howe about his book *Doctor Who A Book of Monsters*. Over four pages are pictures of "a sorry hunch of monsters", including Alpha Centuri, the Candyman, Yeti, Cybermen, Sea Devils, Daleks and Sontarans. Howe himself is not afraid to affectionately laugh at some of the low-budget monsters.

Hopefully both my Greatest Living Englishmen pieces make a contribution to keeping *Doctor Who* alive in the public consciousness, as *Loaded* is selling half a million copies per issue. Other writers are mentioning *Doctor Who* too and it still remains part of the cultural zeitgeist, as those men in fashionable media glasses have started to refer to it.

But by late 1997 there's still no sign of Series 27. I'm busy reviewing each video release and reading *Doctor Who Magazine*. While I've bought a copy of the superb *Doctor Who: The Television Companion* by David J Howe and Stephen James Walker. It has pages of plot analysis for every story ever recorded, even the missing ones, plus memorable quotes, audience ratings, popular myths and lists of the cast and cliffhanger endings. It makes me resolve to watch every episode of *Doctor Who* ever made — and is still by my bedside today.

But there's also a change to my personal circumstances arriving. Nicola brandishes something that looks like the fluid link from William Hartnell's Tardis. And it registers positive. We've been though an adopted cat, now deceased. Now four years into our relationship we're taking a terrifying leap into the unknown. It's my personal cliffhanger. Nicola is pregnant.

This is real life, not *Doctor Who*, and our decision cannot be rewound. Parents have no time to do anything, ever. No more reading the paper, no more loafing in front of the TV, no more eating out or going to the theatre.

Yet the part of me that isn't terrified of responsibility and commitment wants to be a good dad. Someone like Joe Gargery in *Great Expectations* who has larks. A dad who watches tele with his kids and can appreciate fantasy and alien monsters.

Doctor Who will almost certainly never come back. But one day I want to sit down with my future child and watch some old *Doctor Who* videos. She or he will probably think it is rubbish, but if I can just convey something of the magic, the escapism, the silliness, the womb-like interior of the Tardis, and indeed the wobbly scenery, then I will be a happy Whovian dad indeed.

3. DO THE DALEKS, DAD!

Introducing my children to Susan, Soldeed and Silurians on VHS... Kicking pigs and drinking Bishop's Finger with Tom Baker... and the incredible news that Doctor Who is returning.

Having a child proves much easier than going to the National Childbirth Trust classes. The assorted would-be parents form a circle to practice our breathing exercises while our instructress intones a yoga chant designed to induce relaxation during those deep breaths. "Ommmmm..." she chants, "Ommm..." I'm reminded of those ceremonies in *Planet of the Spiders* where Lipton manages to summon up a giant spider to sit on his back. It would be no surprise to end up on Metebilis 3 or even find the Reverend Magister joining in trying to leave a voicemail for Azal. It's less the Sisterhood of Karn and more the Parenthood of Pete.

My daughter Lola is born in the summer of 1998 and for most of the birth I'm behind the metaphorical sofa in the hospital ward, occasionally handing Nicola cups of water. Mercifully the labour is only four hours, my partner is stoic and doesn't swear at me, and not too many moments resemble the organic interior of the Zygons' spaceship. Incredibly we've managed to create a new companion.

Our lives soon become a routine of nappies,

baby-grows, mashed-up broccoli and potato. First I'm wearing a Baby Bjorn sling that looks like one of the more outlandish costumes from *Doctor Who* and then taking trips around the park pushing a McLaren buggy. As Lola grows it's great to rediscover the joys of rolling on the carpet and just playing. We hammer wooden shapes into holes, gaze up at leaves on trees, look for gifts from the fairies in tree trunks, flee from tickle monsters and camp under duvet covers on mum and dad's bed.

My professional life as a freelance journalist carries on, though with more stains on my jumpers than before. *Who* stuff still arrives at *Time Out* and 1999 begins with incredible news filtering through from the Whovian world to the Dad world.

"Doctor Who episode travels in time," reads the *Guardian* story. A missing episode of *The Crusade*, 'The Lion' has been discovered at a film collectors' sale in New Zealand and bought for just $5. For the collector, nothing guarantees obsessiveness better than the knowledge that the collection can never be completed. *Who* Fandom is agog. The National Lottery Show runs a five-minute feature on the discovery.

The finder, Bruce Grenville, reveals that he was quickly contacted by a group of Internet Whovians. He says that when he showed the missing episode, "It was like a really big religious experience for them." It's an amusing description, and I'm tempted to offer up a papier-mâché stalactite and polystyrene rock in Whovian homage myself. I immediately forward the coverage to my pal Cyber Mat Coward in Wiltshire. This gives hope to all of us that those 109 missing Troughton and Hartnell episodes will eventually be found.

The find inspires a number of false rumours. "Celestial Toymaker *not* found in Canada!" reads a news story in *Doctor Who Magazine*, debunking a false internet rumour. Russell T Davies is also mischievously helping to fuel the rumours through his Manchester-set TV series *Queer as Folk*. His Whovian character Vince tells his pal Stuart that he's found a colour copy of episode three of *Planet of the Daleks* (in reality the only copy was in black and white) and the missing fourth episode of *The Tenth Planet* from the same supplier.

In March 1999 there's a much better *Doctor Who* parody on Children In Need's *Doctor Who and the Curse of Fatal Death*, written by one Steven Moffat. It involves actors who you wouldn't mind actually playing the Doctor in Rowan Atkinson, Richard E Grant, Jim Broadbent, Hugh Grant and Joanna Lumley as a female Doctor with Dalek bumps. Jonathan Pryce makes a suitably dastardly Master and Julia Sawalha is a fine companion.

The BBC video contains a behind the scenes documentary in which the likes of Atkinson, Lumley, Pryce and Richard Curtis all confess to being long-term *Doctor Who* fans. Hugh Grant admits that if the BBC brought back the Doctor "I'd definitely be up for it."

I make much of this in my *Midweek* column, suggesting that: *"Spy can already imagine Doctor Hugh being confronted by Daleks and saying 'Ah, right, yes, well, I see, you want to exterminate me, well, that seems pretty bad news but could we, er,*

*perhaps, discuss it over dinner, or something...'
Hugh would be perfect, particularly as after that
infamous incident on Sunset Boulevard, we can
ascertain that he knows all about picking up
unusual companions and asking them to service his
sonic screwdriver. And if Divine Brown isn't up for
the role at his side Spy will happily accept Elizabeth
Hurley at the Tardis console."*

More Whovian treats are on the horizon. The
great Tom Baker is doing a lunchtime signing of his
new children's book, *The Boy Who Kicked Pigs*, at
Waterstone's in Oxford Street in November, 1999.
I'm in at *Time Out* that day, and the editorial team is
informed that I'm off researching an important
story. I'm surprised how nervous I am standing in
the queue. The grown-up part of my persona tells
me there might be a story in this (and there was)
and it might be a good storybook for Lola to read
one day (it was that too). But my inner child just
shouts, "It's the Doctor!"

It's noticeable that Tom has eschewed literary
mineral water in favour of a bottle of Bishop's
Finger. "I get a new bottle for every ten books I
sign," he tells me in his conspiratorial tones. I
mention that I wrote the Greatest Living
Englishman column on him for *Loaded*. "Ah
Loaded! I must say my hairdresser enjoyed all those
references to my ejaculating on film!" he declares.
It seems Baker has confused my piece with a
Loaded feature written by Jon Wilde, that made
extensive reference to the sex scene in his 1972 film
The Canterbury Tales. But as Tom and his
hairdresser are enjoying it so much I don't correct

him.

We have a little chat about his 'grotesque masterpiece' for kids and Baker jokes: "I thought about putting it in the romance section because there are two rats that get on rather well with each other..." Tom then signs my book and I depart a very happy man.

Baker has just appeared as a God-like entity in the re-made *Randall and Hopkirk (Deceased)*. He's good, as he always is, but the performances of Reeves and Mortimer are widely panned.

The Boy Who Kicked Pigs signing is eagerly written about in both my *Time Out* and *Midweek* columns and used as a basis for demanding the return of real *Doctor Who*. The 100,000 readers at London's stations (apart from Russell T Davies if he's on the tube) must be getting a bit fed up with my demands by now, but like the Daleks, I'm going to deviate. My *Midweek* column reads:

"Randall and Hopkirk (Deceased) *was never that popular in the first place. Yet the one programme that still has legions of fans of all generations and a built in regeneration scenario,* Doctor Who, *is ignored by the BBC. Find a lead actor of Baker's stature for Season 27 take it seriously and don't let comedians anywhere near it, and the BBC will have a sure-fire ratings winner."*

Dadhood continues with daily trips to nursery, endless searching for dropped cuddly toys, watching children's TV when Nicola's out and trying to find the time to deliver copy.

Lola starts off watching *Teletubbies* with her Dad and soon I've perfected my "eh-oh!" to greet

Tinky Winky, Dipsy, La-la and Po. More advanced viewing comes with *Maggie and the Ferocious Beast* and *Ruby and Max*. It's a delight to immerse myself in the world of children's TV, while pretending that it is part of interactive parenting. But at least I'm there for my daughter, declaring "Great googly moogly!" in Maggie's Nowhereland whenever required.

In early 2001 my second daughter Nell is born. At three months she develops very bad eczema and we spend a year not sleeping, trying to prevent her from scratching her inflamed skin and buying gloved sleeping suits. It's a stressful time on all fronts and Nicola's flat is suffering from subsidence with huge cracks in the walls that may or may not be cracks in the fabric of time through which alien prisoners can emerge. We are forced to rent a two-bedroomed cottage nearby in Whistler Street while repairs and strapping to the flat are carried out.

We receive some help from our nanny Sharon, who happily enough happens to be a Whovian, which in my mind qualifies her for the job. As *Doctor Who* releases start to turn up at *Time Out* on dvd, I buy a new dvd player and replace some of my prized VHS videos with dvds and offer Sharon my old VHS versions of *Spearhead in Space* and *Vengeance on Varos*. She seems pleased. And as Nicola's compost bin in the tiny garden becomes infested with intrusive fruit flies, I soon start to dream of giant maggots invading the house.

The TV reception is terrible in our new rented house and the only way we can get a decent picture is to sign up to Virgin's cable TV. This is fine with me, as part of Virgin's TV package includes UK Gold, which shows *Doctor Who* on Sunday mornings. This way I can record any stories that I don't have, even if the UK Gold logo is annoyingly stuck in the top left hand corner of the picture.

If I'm really efficient I get up early to press the red button on the video recorder and pause it whenever the adverts come on. Though often it just gets left to record the whole lot, complete with trailers for *The Vicar of Dibley* and adverts for Freedom Finance personal loans, Alliance and Leicester car purchase plans, Claimsdirect.com, Slim-Fast and the National Accident Helpline. Annoyingly you only get a second or two of the dum-de-dum theme tune at the end of each episode before the ads roll. But it's a means of recording *The Pirate Planet, The Power of Kroll, Survival, The Twin Dilemma*, and any other stories not in my collection.

Soon this Whovian will have seen every episode it's possible to see. Not that I'm a complete anorak, you understand. My time isn't spent exclusively with other fans or going to conventions. But seeing everything ever made in 26 seasons seems an attainable goal. And as the great fellwalker Alfred Wainwright once said, every man needs a goal, rather than aimless wandering.

Nicola is working three days a week saving the planet at Friends of the Earth (FoE), and introduces me to Christian, the FoE Webmaster, who is a card-carrying Whovian. I'm not sure how Nicola knows he's a *Doctor Who* fan, perhaps the Cyberman head he keeps in the computer room gave it away.

We bond over Gallifreyan matters and I even get to write a spoof *Doctor Who* sketch for the Friends of the Earth Christmas party, starring Nicola as Nikkala, the Doctor's Companion, and Christian as the (web)Master. The Doctor is, of course, a Friend of the Earth.

Rumours abound in *Doctor Who Magazine*. In late 2002 US actor Tom Selleck is rumoured to be lined up for a 40th anniversary re-make of *Shada*, the Tom Baker story that was never completed because of a BBC camera operators' strike. It's said to be starring Paul McGann as the Doctor with support from James Fox, Andrew Sachs and Lalla Ward, but like a lot of things connected with the Whovian universe, it never materialises.

Lola starts in the reception class at primary school in 2003 and I figure that at nearly five she's old enough not to be too scared by vintage *Doctor Who*. We start to watch some *Doctor Who* videos together; even though Nicola worries she'll be terrified and says that I can deal with Lola when she can't sleep. We watch *The Tomb of the Cybermen* together and she still remembers today the Cybermen bursting out of their Clingfilm tombs, the same scene that affected me at my grandparents' house in Stoke back in 1967.

Adric dies at the end of *Earthshock* and we watch those silent credits. It's also educational, because that's how the dinosaurs were wiped out. Lola enjoys Romana dealing with non-deviating Daleks in *Resurrection of the Daleks* and Tom Baker tackling what appears to be a giant phallus in *The Creature From the Pit*. She takes a liking to

Susan Foreman in *An Unearthly Child* and doesn't seem to mind that it's in black and white.

Here I am instructing Lola in Time Lord history and telling her that their mum is a distant cousin of Lalla Ward who was once a companion and married to Tom Baker, you know. Lola later names our chicken Romana after Ward's character, which I'm impressed by. Only all the time I'm worrying about indoctrinating her in something that will get her laughed at by her peers. A programme that was taken off air in 1989 and seems doomed never to rematerialise. Any modern child will surely laugh at those sets and iffy monsters. Am I flogging a dead Tardis? And why do I want to instill Whovian values into my children? But she seems to like it, pleading, "Do the Daleks, Dad!"

I plug away at *Time Out* and *Midweek* trying to resurrect my childhood. But it's surely doomed. Cyber Mat suggests that perhaps we should just appreciate classic *Who* and accept it will never return and even if it did it might not be any good. Maybe he's right. I'm in my 40s, am I too old for all this?

Then something incredible happens. On Friday September 26 2003 comes the news that every Whovian has dreamed about. There it is on the BBC website: "Cult science fiction series *Doctor Who* is returning to TV 14 years after it was axed."

Nicola wonders why I'm shouting at the computer. There's a strange feeling in my stomach. The years of exile, the people who said it would never happen, the patronising comments, the laughter... Yeeeeeees!!! Michael Grade, we gave your boys one hell of a beating! New *Doctor Who*. New blooming *Who*! Captain Yates, I could do with a pint...

My London Spy column in *Midweek* has a suitably triumphant tone: *"For 14 long years we Whovians have been derided. We might have been entombed, but we knew we would emerge and take our place as the supreme power in the Universe! Now comes complete and utter vindication. The BBC has announced that it is bringing back Doctor Who in 2005 for a series scripted by Queer As Folk writer Russell T Davies. Davies is a huge* Who *fan, and in* Queer As Folk *had his character Vince quite sensibly choose his lovers on the criteria of how much they knew about* Doctor Who. *Alan Davies is one of the early favourites to play the Doctor, while other promising candidates include Jonathan Pryce and Richard E Grant. Spy suggests John Simm as an outside bet to become a Scally Doctor, perhaps Leslie Grantham as a dodgy Doctor, and maybe even David Morrissey, so effective as a brooding Gordon Brown in* The Deal, *as a moody Doctor. But whoever gets the role one thing is certain. The Doctor is back and the TV universe has been saved."*

Looking at that piece today it seems rather prescient. Pulling names from the air I've mentioned John Simm, later to become the Master and David Morrissey, destined one day to play *The Next Doctor* in a Christmas special.

In October 2003 I review *Invasion of the Dinosaurs*, the last VHS release of fully-available Doctor Who stories. It has a strong ecological theme, but is always remembered by fans as the one with the crap dinosaurs. I play Nicola some of the relevant green dialogue to impress upon her that the Doctor was a forerunner of Friends of the Earth. The BBC has run out of videos – so they must be thankful they can carry on releasing Who on this new-fangled dvd format and even something called blue-ray.

Time Out's chief sub-editor Nigel Kendal goes to live in Japan and bestows his entire *Doctor Who* video collection on me. Finally I get to see again *Doctor Who and the Silurians* again (I can remember playing at Silurians in primary school) and *Image of the Fendahl.*

My cupboards are indeed bulging with myriad *Who* videos and my companion would gladly see them dematerialise. But I refuse to let them fall into the hands of the Master even if it will take a Tardis to store them in and a division of UNIT to move them if we ever manage to buy a house together.

The excitement grows throughout 2004. The casting of Christopher Eccleston and Billie Piper has my approval in *Midweek*. *"Spy applauds the BBC's choice of Christopher Eccleston as the new* Doctor Who. *Eddie Izzard would have been too silly and Alan Davies too curly. The character has always benefited from being a leftfield choice like Eccleston. Tom Baker was an unknown when he took on the role and Jon Pertwee was only seen as a comic actor before becoming the Doctor. Eccleston has just the right large-lugholed alien persona; he was superb as the spooky psycho accountant in* Shallow Grave *and as a Mancunian Jesus in* The

Second Coming. *Spy's Tardis console is already juddering at the thought of the Doctor's return."*

A sign appears in the heavens too: the discovery of a tenth planet in the Solar System, named Sedna and loitering beyond Pluto. This was, of course, exactly what happened in the William Hartnell-era story *The Tenth Planet*. Could the mysterious new planet be Mondas, the Earth's twin planet which is now the home of the Cybermen? The evidence suggests that workers at Antarctic research stations should keep 'em peeled for tall silver men with body stockings over their faces and truck lamps on their heads.

Lola and her dad carry on with their furtive VHS watching, and sometimes three-year-old Nell sneaks a peek too. On days when Lola is off school with a sore throat we came to a secret pact that as long as we don't tell mummy we can watch the Doctor. Lola detects a family resemblance when Romana glares and shouts "Despicable worm!" at the co-pilot in *The Horns of Nimon*. Graham Crowden's over-the-top performance becomes a family catchphrase as we coo, "Lord Nimon, it is I, Soldeed..." As does the Captain's "Moons of Madness!" from *The Pirate Planet*. In fact I'd been using catchphrases for years without realising, muttering a Peter Davison-like "Brave heart..." whenever a knee was cut or a child had to go to a new school or nursery.

Romana heads off into e-space at the end of *Warrior's Gate*, but we turn to McCoy-era *Who* and decide that Ace is a sensible role model for young schoolchildren. *The Curse of Fenric* becomes a family favourite, as do the scary clowns in *The Greatest Show in the Galaxy*. I introduce my daughter to the giant maggots in *The Green Death*, the Brigadier and UNIT chaps, Captain Mike Yates, the closet eco-hippy, and Sergeant Benton having to lay on a jeep. Whenever we have a happy accident we declare "Serendipity!" in the style of Professor Cliff Jones.

As 2004 moves on Christian from Friends of the Earth watches some of the filming in Swansea and comes back with reports of seeing Simon Callow as Charles Dickens. This sounds promising. Rumours suggest there might be flying Daleks, now that a copyright dispute with the estate of Terry Nation has been resolved. Russell T Davies says all the right things and is planning to produce a ~~serious~~ show at the proper time of Saturday night.

But there's still the fear that it might only appeal to middle-aged men. Are the internet and mobile phone generation ever going to go for it? Christian burns me a dvd of the first show, *Rose*, which he's managed to get off the internet. I'm not going to play it to my children, but can't resist inserting it into my dvd player and looking at it myself. And I'm impressed. It might work... it might actually work.

4. RESURRECTION OF THE WHOVIANS

The Doctor returns in a leather jacket and he's fantastic… mentioned in dispatches by the Brigadier.

❛❛*Doctor Who* Returns!" reads the Biro entry in my desk diary for Saturday March 26 2005. My parents' generation remembered where they were when President Kennedy was shot in 1963. Though as every Whovian knows, JFK was shot on the day before the first ever episode of *Doctor Who* on November 23. But now it's our own JFK moment and no fan will ever forget their location in time and space when the Doctor's Tardis rematerialises at 7pm.

We're in the deepest countryside of north Yorkshire staying with Nicola's friends Richard and Fleur. They're not classic Whovians — Richard is a barrister who enjoys heraldry and hounds and wearing yellow cords, while Fleur is an anthropologist in a tweed jacket who spends her days controlling a tribe of four boys and moving horse boxes down country lanes. Much of the weekend has been spent saddling up ponies and trekking through the muddy fields around Bolton Castle as the girls go riding. Tomorrow Richard is playing the organ at church, but tonight we experience a different kind of resurrection in these secluded environs.

I've mustered support from seven-year-old Lola

and four-year-old Nell plus Fleur and Richard's boys Ned, Jasper, Thomas and George, who are always keen to get in front of the TV when they're not hitting each other. We sit on two sofas. There's a bottle of Black Sheep on hand in case it goes badly.

And here comes musical director Murray Gold's pumped-up, ballsier version of Ron Grainer's classic *Doctor Who* theme. We're racing down a red time vortex tunnel. This is it, it's on TV... we've waited 16 years entombed in terrestrial and then satellite TV history. Do my children notice their over-emotional dad look a little moist-eyed as the famous theme plays again? Dum-de-dum, dum-de-dum... My dread is that they'll think the new *Who* is rubbish and their dad a loser addicted to wobbly scenery and men in bad rubber suits.

Russell T Davies has indeed updated the show, but thankfully it's retained the feel of proper British *Doctor Who*. Christopher Eccleston looks great in his leather jacket and sounds more northern than any other Doctor – though time and space must get a bit cold with only a V-necked jumper on under your jacket. He veers from a wide goofy grin to moments of manic earnestness. When Eccleston gives that speech about feeling the earth revolving through space at a thousand miles an hour he really does sound alien. He forgets about the real Mickey when he's replicated by Autons and talks about the human race as "stupid apes". This could be good.

A radio alarm goes off. Rose lives on a chavvy London council estate in London and works in a department store. Her character is nicely fleshed out. We get to meet her feisty mum Jackie and her nice but slightly useless boyfriend Mickey, one of the first central characters in *Who* to be black. A lot happens quickly, and it's all much pacier than old *Who*. Good use is made of the store's basement full of shop window dummies that start to move with a convincing sound of straining plastic. And we don't even see the Doctor until Rose is about to be killed.

"Nicola, there's a green reference, did you hear that bit about the world being full of toxins for the Nestene Consciousness to feed on?" I declare to my green partner.

I'm not sure about the plastic wheelie bin swallowing Mickey or the Doctor being throttled by a disembodied mannequin's arm, which all seems a bit too silly. But Clive, the anorak character pursuing the Doctor via the internet, is a nice spoof of the real-life online Whovian community. You can tell it's been written by a fan. When Clive the comedy computer geek/conspiracy theorist is shot by a dummy, it's both unexpected and shocking.

The Time War is mentioned for the first time, though not by name. There's a reprise of the famous Auton mannequins bursting out of shop windows scene (in the original we only heard the crash of breaking glass) and a denouement set around the London Eye. Though should the new series be relying on old monsters? Rose swings across a rusty chain to save the Doctor and ends up ditching dull working and eating for danger in the Tardis. And then a trailer — that's a new development — promises the end of the world next Saturday.

None of the children leave the room or ask to

switch channels. After it's over Lola talks about the "Nesting Consciousness" which is, I think, a far superior version of the Nestene Consciousness. I pour another Black sheep and sit contentedly in my armchair.

Even Nicola admits, "the new Doctor is quite good looking." And we later find that it's amassed a massive 10.81 million viewers. That's a sixth of the population of the UK.

Yet all the old doubts return four days later, when it's revealed that Eccleston is leaving at the end of the series. Is *Doctor Who* doomed to fold after just one series? I exchange worried e-mails with Cyber Mat Coward and Christian the Whovian, who all feel that Eccleston is being frankly a bit actor-ly about his fear of being typecast.

My London Spy column in *Midweek* deals firmly with the matter, reading: "After just one series of *Doctor Who* Christopher Eccleston has announced that he's quitting the role for fear of being typecast. Tom Baker gave us seven years! An actor's career is nothing compared to the greater good of saving humanity. Doesn't he realise that the Doctor is the greatest role in modern drama? The new Doctor — rumoured to be Casanova actor David Tennant — must be locked in to a long-term contract under the Shadow Proclamation."

Thankfully it's announced on April 16 that there will definitely be a second series and that Eccleston will be replaced by an actor called David Tennant, who has just starred in *Casanova*. Cyber Mat emails to say that Tennant played a policeman in a radio version of *Dixon of Dock Green* and is a good actor, so that will do me. Though the problem is that as the series progresses Eccleston is starting to be a fantastic Doctor, yet we've already lost him

The second story *New Earth* has some interesting new aliens like The Face of Bo, scuttling robot spider creatures, and Cassandra, a face on a piece of skin who wants to be constantly moisturised in a fine satire of the *Heat* generation's body obsession. And I'm able to tell Nicola that the Doctor says we humans overcome climate change, so she's not wasting her time. Though I do have to break the news to my children that the Earth will indeed be swallowed up by the Sun in several billion years' time and that humanity will die out unless we can colonise alien worlds. A bit much to take in on a Saturday evening.

Nell sits on my knee for *The Unquiet Dead,* as she's a little scared by corpses becoming animated by mysterious blue gas. Simon Callow is an excellent Dickens, just as Christian, who watched the filming in Swansea, said he would be. We enjoy Mr Dickens' bafflement when the Doctor says he's "a fan."

The news series gives me a good London angle (not that I need much excuse) for writing about the Doctor in *LAM* magazine. *Rose*, the first episode of the new *Who* had red buses, shots of Piccadilly Circus, Trafalgar Square, the Tardis materializing on the Embankment, Billie Piper working in a department store based on Harrods, council estates, tower blocks, shop mannequins coming alive in a London shopping centre and the London Eye being used to broadcast messages from the Nestene

Consciousness. So the freebie mag is treated to my top ten *Doctor Who* moments in London, which in case you want to know are:

> 1. Nestene Consciousness using the London Eye as a giant transmitter.
> 2. Shop window dummies murdering humans in Knightsbridge.
> 3. Daleks on Westminster Bridge.
> 4. Cybermen emerging from sewers outside St Paul's Cathedral.
> 5. Yetis in the Underground beneath Covent Garden station.
> 6. Dalek time portal in Shad Thames.
> 7. Dinosaurs all over central London.
> 8. Giant rats in Victorian sewers near Limehouse.
> 9. Mad computer in the Post Office Tower.
> 10. Master abducting Concorde flight from Heathrow and transporting it back to prehistoric times.

My feature suggests that Ken Livingstone, the Mayor of London, should surely be thinking about employing UNIT to guard the Greater London Authority building.

It's when *Dalek*, the fourth story of the new series, airs on April 30 that this fan starts to believe *Doctor Who* — my knackered old cult show — is going to be a huge success. Robert Shearman's brilliant writing makes us have sympathy for a Dalek. Now that's character development. I worry about the children seeing the torture scenes with Simmons, that nasty man in a boiler suit, and the screaming Dalek. It's all a bit Guantanamo Bay. But Christopher Eccleston is brilliant, veering from a loopy grin to uncontrolled rage against the chained Dalek. We learn how the Daleks and the Time Lords were destroyed in the Time War. So the Doctor is the last of his race. And Eccleston goes a bit psycho on us, as we glimpse the Doctor's pain at seeing his race destroyed. Clearly the grief counsellors on Gallifrey were killed too as the Doctor appears to have post-traumatic stress syndrome and unresolved anger issues.

Doctor Who is always at its best when it reflects the concerns of its era, and here it's fear of the new internet. Henry Van Staten, computer nerd turned evil collector of aliens who wipes sacked employees memories, is a splendid parody of the new Silicon Valley internet entrepreneurs. The Doctor tells Van Staten that he'd get on well with the Daleks' creator, who was also a genius. He rages that Van Staten, the man who owns the internet, wants to reduce the stars to his level.

Rose sees an alien side to the Doctor that is truly scary. It's left to Rose to show sympathy to the tortured Dalek and to point out that it's the Doctor pointing a gun at her. Plus we have a levitating Dalek, with a proper menacing voice by Robert Briggs, downloading the entire internet and then revealing the blobby tentacled creature inside, complete with convincing white slime. It's brilliant – and better than we could ever have hoped for. When the Dalek exterminates people you see their skeletons for a second and it also manages to sucker its torturer Simmons to death.

In the aftermath of the questionable legality of the United States and Britain's invasion of Iraq, my *Midweek* column wonders if the Doctor might be breaking the Geneva Convention:

"Is the Doctor guilty of war crimes? During an otherwise excellent episode of Doctor Who *Spy was a little shocked to see the Doctor lose it and attempt to exterminate an imprisoned Dalek. The Dalek was in the hands of an American megalomaniac Internet owner and had been detained and tortured for 50 years without access to a lawyer or being charged with any offence.*

There were also some troubling references to the Time War when the rest of the Time Lords and the Daleks were wiped out. No one knows if this Time War was legal. Leaked documents from the Panopticon may well suggest that the Time Lords had been warned that a pre-emptive war to counter the Daleks' weapons of mass destruction was of dubious legality under intergalactic law.

Is it enough for the Doctor to say, "trust me" on this one? Should concerned Doctor Who *fans protest by switching off or is that woolly liberal self-indulgence? Admittedly the Doctor has done a lot of good in other areas of the universe, but the issue of inhuman rights violations against Daleks will not go away. Spy is so concerned that he is planning on writing a letter to the* Gallifrey Guardian. *"*

Another bonus of the new era is that immediately after *Doctor Who* is broadcast you can switch over to BBC3 and watch *Doctor Who Confidential*, where the writers, directors and cast talk through the scripts and stunts with lots and lots of background information. We become addicted, though invariably I have to video it on my creaking VHS recorder as it's time for dinner once the main programme has finished.

When *Aliens of London* is screened I'm away at my soon-to-be brother-in-law Drew's stag weekend on Islay. We're doing a tour of Scottish whisky distilleries and whizzing around Islay and Jura in a hired speed boat, dodging whirlpools in a speed boat. The pilot is giving it some knots and suddenly the boat has its windscreen smashed by a renegade wave and our party is drenched in salty water. But we're dried-off and in the bar at our hotel in Port Ellen, Islay, when the *Doctor Who* opening credits come on to the bar's TV screen. I'm reminded of those 1970s years when *Doctor Who* was part of the national Saturday night fabric and bulky old TVs on pub walls offered your only chance of catching Tom Baker if you were out of the house. We can't hear the sound but there's an intriguing glimpse of an alien spaceship crashing through Big Ben and into the Thames.

Later that week, back in London having recovered from the whisky overload, catch-up TV reveals the full *Aliens of London* and the following Saturday sees the second part of the Slitheen two-parter, *World War Three*. I like the way Russell T Davies enjoys dealing with the conundrum of how companions explain their absence. Rose has been gone for a year and Mickey has been accused of her murder, while her furious mum Jackie accuses the Doctor of being a well-dodgy older man.

The farting Slitheen provide some lavatory humour for juvenile dads and their kids as they experience problems with the gas exchange, while the unzipping of faces provides us with a ready made family game of 'expose the Slitheen' as I try to unzip my daughters' masks.

The following week's story features Simon Pegg, no longer *Shaun of the Dead*, but now a creepy editor in *The Long Game*, followed by an episode centring on Rose dealing with time paradoxes when she tries to save her father Pete's life in *Father's Day*.

Bizarrely Nicola's brother Andrew decides to get married to Kate on a Saturday that clashes with both *Doctor Who* and the FA Cup Final. They were surprised when that Saturday the church happened to free in an otherwise fully booked summer, little realising that no-one gets married on the day *The Empty Child* is screened.

Thankfully catch-up TV reveals the full glory of one of the finest ever stories in the history of the series. In *The Empty Child* and *The Doctor Dances* writer Steven Moffat beautifully utilises the sinister quality of world war two gas masks. The two episodes are filmed entirely at night and are full of fear for what might lurk in the darkness. Richard Wilson is superb in his role as the troubled Doctor at Albion Hospital. We're also introduced to the matinee looks of the libidinous Captain Jack Harkness, who makes a splendid foil to the Doctor and flirts with anyone in the cosmos regardless of species or gender. *Doctor Who* has come a long way since the asexual days of William Hartnell.

We had no right to expect anything so good as *The Empty Child*. And we get to learn about nanogenes. No need to read Nicola's copies of *New Scientist* anymore to keep up with the latest developments in medicine.

The girls and I spend a lot of time shouting up the stairs at my long-suffering wife, "Mummy, are you my mummy?" Or I push open the children's bedroom doors and walk in, arms outstretched, repeating our new catchphrase. I can't do it late at night though, as it terrifies the children too much. If the social workers call round I'll just rely on the rather more optimistic, "Everybody lives!"

Russell T Davies is writing a column at the back of *Doctor Who Magazine* and he makes the very funny comment that now when you take a new partner home, you no longer have to hide your Dalek.

There's a time rift in Cardiff and the return of the Slitheen in *Boom Town* and then a two-part finale of *Bad Wolf* and *Parting of the Ways*. *Bad Wolf* shows just how inventive the new series is, taking the Doctor into an unparalleled parody of reality TV on Satellite 5, with lethal versions of *Who Wants To Be A Millionaire, Big Brother* and Trinny and Susannah's *What Not To Wear*. It turns out the eliminated contestants are actually being beamed onto a Dalek spaceship where they are filleted for the one per cent of their cells that make a Dalek.

Religious Daleks is a lovely idea and Russell T must have had great fun making them clamping down in blasphemy. Whereas once the Daleks mimicked the certainties of both the non-deviating left and conservative right in the 1970s, post-World Trade Centre attacks they now reflect the fanaticism of religious fundamentalists. Only they're in denial about being half-human too. The fanboy in Russell T assembles just the sort of battle children of my generation used to imagine while creating Lego universes in the 1960s — a God-complex giant Emperor Dalek based on the one in *The Evil of the Daleks*, thousands of flying Daleks, a massed fleet of spaceships and good people like Linda and Captain Jack getting exterminated.

Perhaps Davies makes it a little too sentimental when Rose looks into the Time Vortex, but that would be a minor quibble. I have to explain to the girls that it's OK when the Doctor kisses Rose, as although it's yucky he's simply taking the energy of the Time Vortex into himself in order to save her life. The regeneration is handled well, with lots of orange energy gushing into Eccleston. And then he changes into David Tennant...

"But he's turned into a Beatle!" sobs Lola. Oh no. Showing her those old Beatles pictures has clearly misfired. A Time Lord with Paul McCartney sideburns is too much of a departure for my daughter.

"It's OK, your first regeneration is always difficult," I reassure her. "I was upset when William Hartnell changed into Patrick Troughton... and when Jon Pertwee became Tom Baker."

"But it won't be the same..." sobs my eldest Whovian daughter.

"Is Captain Jack really alive?" asks Nell. "And can we have our pizza now?"

Never before have I had to use so many parenting skills. It's been emotional. But Series 1, as they insist on calling it when it's actually Series 27, has been an undoubted triumph, Beatles lookalikes notwithstanding. It's June 18 and we now have to wait until the promised Christmas Special to see Tennant in action. Luckily I have recorded all the shows on VHS video so we can watch them again and they'll soon be released on dvd, which looks tempting...

Amazing things happen when I drop the kids off at school. Children are shouting "Exterminate!" in the playground and role-playing as companions. Lola has her classmates playing at being Ace and Romana as well as Rose. Nell has just started primary school and is drawing the Tardis and Daleks with elongated arms. The formula still works...

That summer we buy a sonic screwdriver toy for Lola's birthday. It has an extendable end and when you press a button on the side a blue light glows and it makes a beeping sound. I point the sonic screwdriver at the kids' heads in bed, press the button that makes it go bleep and announce: "Small humanoid female detected..."

There are more Whovian delights that year. Through my footie pal Nigel Morris I've started watching games at West Ham with Michael McManus. "He's a complete Whovian too," explains Nigel, "and he's mates with the Brigadier."

Michael is very happy to discuss all matters

Gallifreyan over a pint of tea and full fried breakfast in Ken's Café and it turns out he's written *Still Getting Away With It*, the autobiography of Nicholas Courtney. He's also a regular drinking companion of Courtney's at his local in Crouch End.

When I receive a review copy of *Still Getting Away With It*, I'm astonished to find that Nick mentions me in his introduction. He writes: *"In November 1996 Brigadier Alastair Lethbridge-Stewart – the character I first played in* Doctor Who *back in 1967 – was featured in Loaded magazine as one of the series of Greatest Living Englishmen – for men who should know better. I was astonished; from what little in knew about this periodical I had understood its focus to be all about chaps in the prime of their lives not aging thespians. Yet here was a writer called Pete May hailing dear old Alastair as 'the man for all invasions. The greatest ever living English chap to fire five rounds rapid at that chap with the wings.' It was all very funny and my wife was at once amused and appalled, for better or worse I appear to have played my part in the creation of a modern-day icon. It is quite a thought."*

It's a proud moment and possibly the highlight of my career. Mentioned in dispatches by the Brigadier! Honorary membership of UNIT can't be far off. The Introduction is followed by a Foreword by Tom Baker.

Michael holds the launch party for *Still Getting Away With It* at the Club for Acts and Actors in Bedford Street, Covent Garden, reached through an inconspicuous doorway. Attempting to give my now eight-year-old daughter Lola a good start in life I take her along. Never mind soft skills learned at private schools, she'll have met Whovian royalty.

It's an old-fashioned actorly private bar, all dark-stained wood and portraits on the wall. Nick Courtney, fuller of figure these days and with a white beard replacing the Brig's moustache, is resplendent in braces and purple shirt.

Michael introduces both myself and Lola to Nick and I have the chance to personally thank him for the mention in the introduction, before he's ushered on to meet the legendary *Who* scriptwriter Terrence Dicks, who's drinking a pint of bitter.

Both Michael and Nick make speeches and then there's a signing session with Nick sitting at a table surrounded by piles of purple-tinted autobiographies. I get a "best wishes" from Nick while Michael writes, "The introduction is great, but it goes downhill from there!'

We mingle among the Who-ocracy and Lola is impressed to see the real life Ace in Sophie Aldred. We rush over, "Excuse me Sophie, this is my daughter Lola and she's a big fan of Ace, would you mind signing an autograph for her please," I declare, omitting to reveal my own fandom. Sophie signs a page of Lola's notebook and we later frame it and place it on Lola's bedroom mantelpiece.

That appears to be Wendy Padbury over there. And Elisabeth Sladen and Katy Manning. "See that man over there, he's a *Doctor Who* legend and a really nice man," whispers Michael. And there's an elderly white-haired man drinking on his own called

William Russell. Chesterton, dear boy! I'm in the same room as the man who pulled Barbara (possibly) and managed to combine being knighted by Richard 1 with climbing inside an empty Dalek casing on Skaro during his spell in the Tardis. We then have to go home as it's Lola's bedtime, but spotting Ian Chesterton seems a good note to go out on.

Meanwhile the time has arrived to cement my own companion status. It's been such a good year on the Whovian front that in December Nicola and I decide to get married. And I had previously offered her a marriage voucher redeemable on any year in which *Doctor Who* returned. Though admittedly she might not place so much emphasis on Time Lord matters. Sadly my mum has been diagnosed with Alzheimer's Disease and another reason for our decision is that we want to be married while she can still remember the day. But the children are keen to be bridesmaids too and it's hard to ignore the feelgood portents. If you can't do it in the year when the Doctor returns when can you?

Stephen the vicar manages to mention the Tardis in his wedding ceremony, claiming that marriage is bigger on the inside than out, which is probably a first in the history of St Thomas's Church. We go to Lille for a short honeymoon having secured three days of childcare and return in time for the festive season. I guess we'll always have Lille... and there's *The Christmas Invasion* to come too.

Doctor Who is given the status it deserves with a 60-minute primetime slot on Christmas Day – the first Christmas Special in its history, if we discount the live episode *The Feast of Stephen* in *The Daleks' Master Plan*. We watch it while staying with Nicola's mother's house in Bishop's Stortford, the children having insisted that everything has to stop for the early evening broadcast.

David Tennant looks cool in his converse trainers and computer geek suit. Lola decides that having a Beatle in the Tardis might not be too bad. Deadly Santa robots and scary Sycorax invaders, plus Harriet Jones from the Slitheen stories as Prime Minister and the Doctor in pyjamas, make for an enticing mix. Tennant is lighter and more garrulous than Eccleston, but he is agreeably manic and thoroughly convincing in the role. The kids gasp as the Doctor's hand is scythed off by the Sycorax commander, but luckily it regrows as he's in the first 15 hours of his regeneration. And then, after Harriet Jones destroys the Sycorax spaceship in a reprise of the Brigadier's love of big bangs, the Doctor manages to end her career as Prime Minister simply by suggesting she looks tired. Tennant is going to be great.

It's a suitable end to 2005 and *The Christmas Invasion* is watched by 9.84 million viewers. The Doctor has been regenerated in every sense.

5. THE DOCTOR WILL SEE YOU NOW

*Eggsterminating boiled eggs… monster stickers…
fending off gas mask creatures… and an audience with
David Tennant.*

We begin 2006 with much egg-sterminating of boiled eggs. The girls have received a radio-controlled Dalek battle pack, consisting of one black and one gold Dalek and a model of Christopher Eccleston. The Daleks are great for both 46-year-old men and children to play with. Hand-held controls allow them to move across the floor and they talk too. When you press the button the Daleks fire at each other. Score a few hits and the Dalek dies with a convincing scream.

The radio-controlled Daleks are easily adapted when eating boiled eggs for breakfast. Before slicing the top off the girls' eggs I point a Dalek at the egg and croak, "Egg-sterminate! Egg-sterminate!" When the shell is sliced off with a teaspoon my Dalek says, "My shell is impaired my shell is impaired… Aaaaaaaargh!"

Inevitably, given the roughness of children's make-believe games, one of the Daleks' eyepieces eventually breaks off. Though I guess we can pass it off as collateral damage obtained in the Time War.

Series 2 of the new *Doctor Who* begins on April 15 with *New Earth*, which is a little underwhelming, but there's no denying that Tennant is a brilliant

Doctor. He's more flippant and funny than the old Doctor, firing off sentences and technobabble, whipping out his sonic and generally up for a laugh and an adventure in his computer geek suit, but able to switch to an impressive other-worldly anger too.

From then on it gets better and better. Nell sits on my knee and is particularly scared of the werewolf menacing Queen Victoria in *Tooth and Claw*. I help my kids hide behind the sofa and cope with *Doctor Who*-induced night terrors, while insisting to Nicola that of course they're old enough to watch it.

Lola has read *Doctor Who* magazine and tells me excitedly that K9 and Sarah Jane are returning in *School Reunion*. We watch with great anticipation. Russell T Davies gives the story real emotional depth as we learn the disappointment felt by the companions the Doctor has left behind. There's a nice initial rivalry between Rose and Sarah Jane, or "the missus and the ex" as Mickey puts it. As the treasurer of my children's' primary school PTA I also love the idea of the teachers being Krillitanes and sleeping upside down from the ceiling on the top floor. I tell the girls to check for signs of aliens in the staff room at school on Monday. For several weeks Lola walks around the house repeating the Doctor's line, "K9! He recognises me!"

A week after *School Reunion* is broadcast, Elisabeth Sladen and John Leeson, the voice of K9, are doing a book signing at the Who Shop in East Ham. I take my daughters before a West Ham home match. We've become regular visitors to the Who Shop, one of those typically obscure London treasures hidden away in the East End, and I manage to sneak a short item on the Who Shop into the Family page of the *Guardian*.

Their mum is opposed to TV toys and says kids should make their own entertainment — but hey, she doesn't know about Slitheens with moveable arms or toy metal spiders. We enter the shop, close to East Ham tube, and the girls are delighted to find David Tennant figures, movie Daleks, *Doctor Who* novels published by Target, Cybermen t-shirts, *Who* pencil cases, Tardis cookie jars, a back issue of *Doctor Who Magazine* with a Lalla Ward interview, model Sontarans and a piece of a real Cyberman blaster behind a glass case.

Lola is pleased to find a queue of *Doctor Who* 'raincoats' (her term for anoraks) and discusses the merits of Tom Baker versus David Tennant with another eight-year-old. Finally we enter the Time Lord temple itself and edge towards Sladen and Leeson.

"Lola and Nell, what lovely names!" exclaims Elisabeth Sladen/Sarah Jane as she signs a photo for my pair of happy Whovians. She still looks remarkably young and I ask her if her daughter enjoyed watching her return on *Doctor Who*, which she did.

"Thank you Daddy," says five-year-old Nell. "Can I have a remote-controlled K9 too?" We frame the signed picture of Sladen and David Tennant's Doctor looking inside K9 and place it on the girls' mantelpiece.

The importance of the new *Doctor Who* reveals itself when I'm playing for my pub quiz side, the

Beta Males. *Doctor Who* questions frequently come up and with a fellow Whovian David from Sotheby's also in the team, we normally have all matters *Who* sorted. Our captain, my old mate Bob, not normally a Whovian, starts raving about the mythic quality of *The Girl In the Fireplace* and how beautifully written it was. With its themes of childhood, time passing and returning figures in fireplaces was it a Christian allegory? Written by Steven Moffat it's one of the finest ever *Doctor Whos*. The clockwork robots under courtiers' costumes, lurking beneath the bed, is a brilliant idea, while Sylvia Miles is beautifully vulnerable as Madam de Pompadour.

Redesigned Cybermen return in the two-parter *Rise of the Cybermen/The Age of Steel*. I like their voices and synchronised stomping, though they appear to be wearing flares and look a little too muscle-bound for this old Whovian. Though controlling people through earpieces again brings the programme right up to date with modern life.

The Idiot's Lantern sees David Tennant with a quiff. It feels close to home for us, as it features Alexandra Palace and Muswell Hill. Nicola is proved right about TV rotting brains and indeed faces. Was she tipped off about the Wire? While growing up in the 1960s I recognise the Little Englander character of Eddie "I am talking!" Connolly.

The Doctor leaves Earth to loiter around a Black Hole in a scary two-parter *The Impossible Planet/The Satan Pit*. It's an updated 'base-under-siege' story but beautifully done. *Doctor Who* appeals because it's human drama set among the big questions and huge distances of the Universe. And those signs appearing on their faces are terrifying...

Love and Monsters is silly but Peter Kay is funny as the Absorbalof and it gives is another catchphrase of "tastes like chicken!" And it features an absorbed Shirley Henderson, who's Moaning Myrtle in the *Harry Potter* films, which impresses my children.

The series ends with the first ever confrontation of the Daleks and Cybermen in *Army of Ghosts/Doomsday*, with the Daleks winning on a TKO. You can bet Russell T played that game with his Lego as a kid. The ghosts idea is excellent and Davies includes an alternative universe with a brave Mickey as a possible homage to *Inferno*. He ladles on the sentiment as Rose departs, complete with mushy music, but we'll forgive him that. The beach scene looks great, though Lola and Nell are relieved Rose is leaving because there is too much snogging and it's yucky.

And that's it, another triumphant series over on July 8. How could I have ever doubted its success? But it's not the last we've seen of the Doctor.

A week later comes an opportunity to actually meet David Tennant. Our local paper reveals that Tennant is doing a signing at the Ashmount School Fete in north London, where his godson, the daughter of the actress Arabella Weir, is a pupil. It's only a week since Series 2 finished. No-one can quite believe it. Nell and Nicola are away for the weekend but I'm there, determined for Lola to meet the Doctor. It's a very hot day which will be good for attendance, possibly too good — we find a huge queue snaking along the pavement outside the school gates.

We pay our 50p entry fee and find record numbers of parents and children desperate for an audience with a Time Lord. The tombola and snag-the-duck stalls must be making record profits. We buy some lunch. There's an excited hubbub as Tennant is spotted entering the playground. He's wearing jeans and a tight white t-shirt with a reindeer on it. Dads with jelly-bellies look on enviously at the trim Time Lord. David is given a microphone and stands under a gazebo and lots of bunting welcoming us to the Ashmount School Fete. Then he's ushered into a school building by Arabella Weir, author of *Does My Bum Look Big in This*?

The children have made an effort to welcome him too. There's a yellow cardboard Dalek on display, predating Steven Moffat's Teletubby Daleks by some years, and a blue cardboard Tardis.

A handwritten sign reads "DOCTOR WHO PHOTO HERE" by the entrance to the main school. You'd have thought someone on the PTA would have known it was the Doctor not Doctor Who, but it's probably best not to point this out.

A huge queue has formed of parents and children desperate to have their photo taken with David Tennant. We meet my old friend Hilary from Red Wedge days and her daughter Florence. Seems a long time now since I was writing my review of *Day of the Daleks* and its critique of Thatcherism for *Well Red,* the magazine that Hil was editing.

Half of London is in the queue and it's looking bad.

Arabella Weir marches to a point halfway down the line. She looks intimidating in the way only a PTA mum can and announces: "Anyone beyond this point won't be able to have their photo taken with David as we can't fit in any more people because of health and safety reasons, there's no point in anyone else queuing, we've had far more people than we thought. I'm very sorry, but please don't wait if you're not in front of this point."

"Lola, we're not moving. We're going to see him whatever it takes!" I tell my daughter. What sort of dad am I if I can't get access to the Doctor for my daughter? I take out the NUJ press card from my wallet and wave it at Arabella.

"I'm doing a piece on David for the Family section of the *Guardian* and I need to get some quotes from him," I lie abjectly. "It would be great publicity for the school."

She appears to sense the desperation in my voice and doesn't throw me out of the queue, possibly because she regards me as dangerous. My own knowledge of being the Treasurer of my daughters' primary school PTA comes in useful here too. The people organising this are harassed middle-class liberal parents who find it difficult to book clowns and organise hook-the-rubber-duck stalls at school fetes at the best of times. There's no way they're going to be able to throw out a determined Whovian Dad.

We make it inside the school. It's even hotter inside. There's a table selling *Doctor Who* novels and *Doctor Who* pictures for £10. You have to buy one to get it signed and also pay a fee to have your photo taken with David.

It feels like waiting for Father Christmas. We purchase the *Doctor Who* novel *The Stone Rose* by Jacqueline Rayner, the first official novel to feature the tenth Doctor, and swelter in an airless corridor. After an interminable queue we are finally ushered in to meet Santa — I mean the Doctor — in a classroom.

Tennant says hello in his natural Scottish accent. "Lola, that's a nice name," he says.

"I don't think you're the last of the Time Lords," says Lola, increasing in confidence. "What about the Doctor's granddaughter Susan and Romana and the Master?'

"Ah, but they could have all been killed in the Time War," counters David.

"Romana went into e-space, she's still alive," suggests Lola. I'm immensely proud of my daughter's knowledge of Whovian lore. Never mind Oxbridge, (William) Russell Group universities and SATS – she can debate with the Doctor! And she has a good point. We can't prove that Tennant ever mentioned Lola's theory to Russell T Davies, but it's surely significant that at the end of Series 3 the following year the Master does indeed return.

Lola must be the umpteenth child that Tennant has dealt with. He looks hot and tired but he's brilliant at handling awestruck 46-year-olds — and pretty good with Lola too. He signs the book and we ask him to dedicate it to Nell too. Lola then poses for a photograph with the Doctor. David places his arm around her and pulls his 500th grin of the day and the event photographer takes the picture and gives us a number, which we will use to collect the picture later.

"Thank you Doctor, I mean David, I know it's been a hot day but you were fantastic…" I stammer. We head out into the sunshine happier than Sontarans at a cloning festival. The fete winds down and we see Tennant being whisked out of the building by Arabella Weir and hopefully being taken to her home for a Douglas Adams-sized Pan-Galactic Gargle Blaster. His godson will certainly be coolest kid in school this week. Inside Lola's book the felt pen message reads: "To LOLA AND NELL David Tennantx"

My mind clicks though previous Doctors that I've got up close and Gallifreyan with: Jon Pertwee at Aldbourne, Tom Baker at Waterstones in Oxford Street, Peter Davison, Sylvester McCoy and Colin Baker at the 30th anniversary celebrations in Hammersmith and now David Tennant. We walk home from the school to Finsbury Park in a triumphant mood.

A week later we collect our photo from a curtain shop at Archway that presumably belongs to someone in the PTA. And there it is — posing with his arm around a disbelieving Lola is a tired but grinning David Tennant. My daughter has met the Doctor.

6. ALLONS-Y! THE TENNANT YEARS

*Not blinking... becoming scared of our own shadows...
Donna goes up West Ham... and experiencing the
Doctor at Olympia.*

Doctor Who features heavily among our
Christmas presents at the end of 2006. The
children receive some Dalek socks (much
cheaper from Woolworths than anywhere else) and
the 2006 *Doctor Who* annual, which features a story
by Steven Moffat called *What I Did On My
Christmas Holidays*, later to form the basis for
Blink. My mind turns to the *Who* annuals I used to
have, particularly the 1966 one with William
Hartnell and the Zarbi on the front, with their
beautiful illustrations and all the pleasure they game
during the lonely days between episodes.

Best of all, Nicola has ordered a five-foot tall
inflatable Dalek that takes forever to blow up with
my bicycle pump. The arms take forever to make
erect and the eyestalk droops slightly but it's big
and its fun. For a time it ends up on the bay window
balcony outside my daughters' bedroom,
threatening our street with a limp plunger arm

Childhood seems more important than ever after
the death of my mother in October. She was taken
ill with a stomach ulcer and a week later died in
hospital. My dad is lost without her and stays with
us in London for Christmas.

My dad doesn't care much about TV, and still

thinks *Doctor Who* is for kids, but on Christmas Day we watch *The Runaway Bride*, which features an excellent performance from Catherine Tait as the stroppy Donna Noble and an over-the-top giant spider, the Empress of the Racnoss.

After that the girls and myself are left waiting for the new series and discussing whether the teachers are all actually Krillitanes on our 20-minute walks to primary school.

Series 3 begins on March 31 2007 and it's another triumph. Early press coverage centres on the fact that Freema Agyeman is to play Martha Jones, the Doctor's first black female companion. Agyeman is great in the role as a university-educated doctor, and my children certainly find her less irritating than Rose's character in her later 'I Love the Doctor' gushy phase, when Russell T Davies ladled on the sentimental endings. Martha's ethnicity is used to bring up issues of racism in stories like *The Shakespeare Code* and *Human Nature*, which adds something new to the mix.

The first episode *Smith and Jones* is promising, with a hospital being transported to the Moon by the Judoon. The Judoon are rhino-like space police that are easy to imitate. I amuse my children by chanting things like "Yo ho ko po to!" at them.

I'm at a football match when *The Shakespeare Code* is broadcast, but Nicola has watched the story with the girls, and having recently taken them to see Shakespeare's Globe, I think she might even be starting to agree that *Doctor Who* is educational. "Martha told Shakespeare he had really bad breath!" declare the children, excitedly.

Large amounts of stickers are given away in *Doctor Who Adventures* and they soon appear all over the kids' bunk beds and on their wooden Trip-Trap chairs in the kitchen. A Judoon, Martha and the Doctor are stuck to the sitting room door. Circular *Who* stickers abound on pine rails whenever I clamber into the children's bunk beds to read them a bedtime story.

In *Gridlock* I'm delighted to find the Macra making reappearance from the 1960s. I tell the children that I've never forgotten that claw appearing on the Tardis scanner and Polly screaming at the end of *The Moonbase*.

Daleks In Manhattan and *Evolution of the Daleks* get a bit silly with the pig slaves (an idea nicked from a Magritte painting?) and Dalek Sec becoming a human Dalek. Though it's undeniably entertaining and the Daleks suit the art deco Empire State Building, as Russell T explains on *Doctor Who Confidential*. *42* has the nice touch of being filmed for 42 minutes in real time, and I like the idea of the Sun creatures, even if one of the parents at school suggests it's a rip-off of Danny Boyle's *Sunshine*.

Series 3 really starts to evolve too with *Human Touch* and *The Family of Blood*. You don't need a bunch of special effects to make *Doctor Who* scary. Just a walking scarecrow appearing at a window or a scary posh boy with jug ears possessed by the Family of Blood. And Harry Lloyd is superb as a pre-Benedict Cumberbatch scary posh boy called Baines.

World war one and the setting of a private school

training boys to fight and die for the British Empire is brilliantly suited to Phil Cornell's plot. And we find a new catchphrase from the Family of Blood as I refer to the kids as "Daughter of mine…"

David Tennant proves he really can act as the Doctor turns himself human via the convenient plot device of the Chameleon Circuit. As John Smith he's constrained, patriotic, very English, and capable of falling in love with a human. His relationship with Jessica Hynes' Matron is one of the highlights of the new generation of *Who*. Smith's look of bafflement at the news he might be a Time Lord is testimony to an astonishing performance by Tennant, as is the scene where he breaks down saying that he just wants to be plain John Smith. And he asks he awkward question of just what sort of man is the lonely Doctor?

Meanwhile there's drama in our house too. Nicola has planned a three-month trip around the UK that she's blogging about under the title of Around Britain No Plane. The plan is we housesit for holidaying friends around the country and rent hostels or hotels on any days when we can't find free accommodation. We've had to take the children out of school six weeks early, agreeing to home educate them. Though their main concern — and mine— is that wherever we are we must be able to watch *Doctor Who*.

We leave London on the night train to Glasgow and our first challenge is to find a TV at Loch Lomond Youth Hostel. Lola is starting to go down with tonsillitis and I'm under strict instructions from Nicola to keep her confined to the family dorm. But Lola's very insistent that she has to watch *Doctor Who* and I manage to sneak her into the TV room with Nell, where we watch one of the best stories ever screened in *Blink*.

What's extraordinary is that the Doctor and Martha hardly appear in it, apart from in a series of messages at the back of Sally Sparrow's dvds. The story is carried by the admirable Carey Mulligan as Sally Sparrow and Finlay Robertson as Kathy's geek brother Larry.

Steven Moffat creates perhaps the scariest monsters of new *Doctor Who* in the Weeping Angels, all set in a *Scooby Doo*-type deserted house. Again no dramatic special effects, just statues that are alive and, apparently, the loneliest creatures in the universe. If you blink they edge closer and kill you by sending you back in time to live yourself to death. Poor Kathy being sent back to Hull in 1920 and sending a message to Sally via her grandson is a genuinely horrific idea. "Don't turn your back. Don't look away. And don't blink!" We scan the shores of Loch Lomond for statues, but for that night our way is clear. It's probably best we share a family room as no-one wants to sleep alone.

For the next episode, *Utopia* — directed by Graeme '*Caves of Androzani*' Harper, which is always a treat — we are in Kettlewell in the Yorkshire Dales, staying with Nicola's friend Anna. It's one of those classically beautiful English villages that seems ripe for alien invasion – only these days the threat is mainly from southerners doing barn conversions says our hostess. As we watch that evening's episode there's a definite frisson at discovering that the Master, played by Derek Jacobi, is alive at the end of the story and the Doctor is not the last of the Time Lords.

We watch *The Sound of Drums* in a rented cottage in Cockermouth in the Lake District. The day before we've celebrated Lola's ninth birthday with tea and jelly babies by the River Derwent.

John Simm is the Master now. He's entered politics as "Mr Saxon" and with his tough choices about universal domination comes across as probably more of a control freak than even Peter Mandelson. Rather worryingly, Nicola finds the manic energy of Simm as the Master rather sexy. Maybe I should start wearing black gloves and calling her "Miss Baird" in the manner of Roger Delgado... though ultimately it's his wife who does for the Master, so maybe not.

For the finale of the series, *Last of the Time Lords*, we've crossed the country to Whitley Bay, where we're staying in or friend Tom's house. The Master has released the Toclafane and enslaved the planet, as you do. Then he's aged the Doctor into a wizened tiny thing in a cage and gets well gleeful, but has reckoned without Martha forcing the whole planet to think of the word Doctor and rejuvenate him, so everything gets to turn out OK and Lucy Saxon shoots the Master. Phew. It's all a bit much to take in at Whitley Bay.

Our travels continue, taking in Wooler, Edinburgh, Dalmally, Aberdeen, Greenlaw and Wakefield. We've been ringing my dad regularly, but shortly after we return, I visit for a few days with my sister and the evening after we leave he has a stroke. I rush to the hospital in time to be with him, but his speech isn't making any sense and he dies the following morning at the age of 80.

There's a funeral, my other sister Pam arrives from Australia along with my younger sister Kaz, and we begin a long year of dealing with wills and clearing my parents' house. Clearing the house unearths some of the detritus of my childhood. Much of it was given away when my parents moved from their farm in 1985, but amid my A level text books and ring folders, a wedge of 1970s concert and football tickets, a book of the lyrics of Bernie Taupin and some Thomas Hardy novels, there's still an old *Doctor Who* annual with Patrick Troughton on the cover and a Piccolo paperback on *The Making of Doctor Who* by Malcolm Hulke and Terrance Dicks. And from my adult years there are old copies of *Midweek* with my *Doctor Who* articles.

As my childhood re-emerges from a spare room in Kings Lynn it's comforting to sit in my own daughters' shared bedroom and see the lovely enthusiasm of childhood, untempered by adult cynicism. A time when TV programmes are almost real and there's a model of K9 on the mantelpiece and a Family of Blood scarecrow sticker on their bunks.

We have to regularly visit my parents' old house in Kings Lynn to keep clearing away their possessions, so much of 2008 and season four is spent watching *Doctor Who* there. It's strangely reassuring to record *Partners in Crime* on my Dad's clunky old JVC video, while watching from the very same sofa — with collapsible sides ineffectually held up by tasseled knobs — from which I watched the programme in the 1970s. I couldn't agree with my dad over politics or career choices, but TV was usually neutral ground. My mum always remembered that I liked *Doctor Who,* but by the time of its return had Alzheimer's Disease and didn't remember recent events, though I told her of my excitement.

The front room speaks of mortality, but also of evenings spent watching Wainwright and *All Creatures Great and Small* visits while drinking home made beer. While I was adrift amid the hostile vortex of the London flatshare market it represented stability and a place to escape to.

Following her effective appearance in the Christmas special *The Runaway Bride* Catherine Tate is Donna Noble, the Doctor's new mouthy companion. We watch the James Moran story *The Fires of Pompeii* while in Norfolk and though we don't know it, it has red-haired Karen Gillan playing a Soothsayer of the Sibylline Sisterhood (a nice nod to the Sisterhood of Karn?) and future Doctor Peter Capaldi playing upwardly mobile sculptor and merchant Caecilius. People's arms turning to stone is a nice touch and the Doctor has to destroy Pompeii to rid the Earth of the Pyroviles, though Donna does persuade him to save Lucius Caecilius' family. It's a fine episode and afterwards Lola and Nell use a felt pen top draw eyes on their hands in imitation of the Sisterhood.

The Friday after *The Fires of Pompeii* is screened it's time to take Lola and Nell to the

Doctor Who Experience at the Earls Court Exhibition Centre (Check). We enter through a black corridor with Auton mannequins standing in alcoves behind wire mesh. We creep past, as slowly the dummies click and bits of them start to move. Don't know about the kids but I'm a bit worried.

There's plenty of monsters on display from the new series, Slitheen, the Face of Bo, Anne Droid, Weeping Angels, the Absorbalof, an Ood spaceship and lots of detail on how the Ood costumes were created. Interestingly the Emperor Dalek that got all religious is quite small, despite appearing huge onscreen.

The Dalek room is of course the scariest and seven-year-old Nell wants to rush past the Daleks and throbbing red backlights. I hold her hand and tell her it will be all right, but actually no it won't. "Life forms detected! They must not reach the Genesis Ark!" says the Dalek in front of us with its lights and eyepiece flashing. "Life forms identified. They are human. You have no purpose. You will be destroyed. Seal all doors.'

There's a series of scary clangs. "Exterminate! Exterminate!" Beams of green light emanate from the Daleks' blasters, which thankfully pass above us perhaps having been designed by a 1980s props man, though just to be safe we rush through the exit.

Outside we meet the Cyber Controller sitting on a huge throne. He tells us we are not compatible and must be deleted. We get to see ourselves in the Tardis via a TV screen and there's a little shop at the end. We end the day with some sandwiches and hot chocolate from the café, where the prices are also astronomical, but it's a great day out and is my contribution to educational parenting over the Easter holidays.

In the third story of the series, *Planet of the Ood* there's an incredible moment — the first mention of West Ham on *Doctor Who*. (West Ham are also the only team mentioned in *Harry Potter*.) The Doctor asks Donna where she learned to whistle like that and she answers "up West Ham!" which has me jumping up in delight.

Football should be used more in *Doctor Who*. The Doctor confessed "I was a dad once," in *Fear Her*, which suggests he might have had the odd kick about on Gallifrey with his child. Football might also be fertile ground for John Sims' Master. He's impersonated a vicar and prime minister in the past and is expert at duping gullible, fearful or ambitious humans by throwing money at them and then reneging on his promises. Perfect material for a Premier League Chairman called Mr Magister perhaps?

The Sontarans return in *The Sontaran Stratagem/The Poisoned Earth* and *Who* proves adept at incorporating another aspect of modern life, Satnav, into something sinister. The trailer that promises *The Doctor's Daughter* has Lola very excited, proving her theory, as espoused to David Tennant, that there must be more Time Lords and Ladies as the Doctor is a grandfather. Georgia Moffat is perfect as Jenny, the Doctor's cloned daughter, and his initial reluctance to acknowledge her gives Donna the chance to chide the Doctor for being a typical man failing to take responsibility.

Jenny's pretty good at cartwheels too, before she disappears into space awaiting her sequel.

The series has other highlights. We watch Steven Moffat's *Silence in the Library* round at Lola's friend Corinna's house and with its skeletons in space suits it's an all time scary episode and make us, literally, scared of our own shadows. "Hey who turned out the lights?" gives me another catch phrase to scare the children with. And they take to a new character called River Song and repeat her "Hello Sweetie!" The second part, *Forest of the Dead,* is a little too complicated and ends up with River Song being subsumed by the Library's mainframe software, or something like that.

Turn Left features Catherine Tate's best performance as she lives life without the Doctor, while Bernard Cribbins is outstanding as her grandfather. His pain at seeing wartime horrors repeated after the Dalek invasion is acting at its best.

We watch *Midnight* up in Norfolk and Nicola says it's a very good piece of writing, which I note down in "my wife appreciates *Doctor Who*" book of treasured remarks.

For the first-part of the two-part finale, *The Stolen Earth*, I'm at Hesdin in France for my friend Katie's 50th birthday party (she's been married to my old Whovian mate Paul since the 1980s). They've hired a house and squeezed 29 old friends into it. Katie and Paul's daughters Emily and Lottie are both New Whovians and they've managed to find BBC on the French TV. All the guests squeeze into the front room to watch the Doctor, including

Nick, my old schoolfriend whose dad used to enjoy the Master so much in Jon Pertwee's day. Karaoke and gratuitous drinking can wait.

Russell T Davies gives it 11 on the Whovian amplifier, gathering together all the characters from spin-offs like *Torchwood* and *The Sarah Jane Adventures* plus Harriet Jones, former Prime Minster. Paul, Nick and myself are delighted by the return of Davros and his twitching mechanical hand while his plot of moving whole planets is properly epic stuff.

The universe is crumbling and the sky is turning black — or is that just the effect of the wine? Scenes of German Daleks terrorising the population will go down into Whovian folklore. While the Doctor is exterminated at the cliffhanger moment and appears to be about to regenerate...

The following Saturday it's our neighbourhood street party, but the girls are absolutely insistent we have to return to the house for *Journey's End*. It gets very sticky for the Doctor as Davros does a lot of mad gloating. Finally the universe is saved by the Doctor's severed hand, a half-human Doctor and Donna becoming Doctor Donna, with the very sad outcome of her memory being wiped and her forgetting everything that ever happened in time and space. Oh, and Russell T Davies finally gets his happy ending with the half human Doctor snogging Rose and going off to fall in love in a parallel universe. Phew.

My mum and dad's house is finally sold in the autumn of 2008 and life moves on. The Tennant era ends with four specials. *The Next Doctor* is the 2008

Christmas special and features David Morrissey, a man who isn't the Doctor but thinks he is.

In 2009 we're restricted to just two specials *Planet of the Dead* (and that fantasy of a London bus being transported to another planet is the sort of thing I've thought about, being a sad Whovian) and *The Waters of Mars*, which sees a darker Doctor.

We learn that a young actor called Matt Smith is to take over and I reassure the girls that having seen him in a series called *Party Animals* I think he's a good actor.

Eight-year-old Nell certainly knows how to impress her dad on April Fool's Day, for I receive a letter reading:

Dear Pete May,

You are the new Doctor Who. You are better than me even! You will be great! You will be famous. I look forward to meeting you, Pete May. Be Good. Signed, The Real David Tennant

PS If you can not read my writing I am not a neat writer.

PPS This is not me writing it is Russell T Davies.

Nell also compiles a "Free Pete May Poster" offer on a piece of A4 paper with the text: "|Matt Smith quits. But good news fans Pete May has started He is better than Matt Smith. Go Pete May." Clearly she deserves an increase in pocket money.

At a car boot sale at the girls' primary school we purchase a Cyberman head for just £2. You press a button and it says, "Delete" and "you must be upgraded". At Halloween I escort my daughters in horror masks and wear the Cyberman head to add to the spookiness.

David Tennant's era finishes with the Christmas 2009 and New Year 2010 Specials. In *The End of Time* the Master recruiting the homeless is a good idea, though it has to be said the goodbyes take a very long time. Tennant regenerates, the girls cry, and I feel a bit odd myself as Matt Smith arrives to say "Geronimo!"

Although there's been a sense of drift with the hiatus in new *Who* — and the first four high quality series are going to be very difficult to follow – Tennant has been immense in the role. He's up there with Tom Baker and Jon Pertwee and to my mind might just be the greatest Doctor. And now Lola tells me he's dating Georgia Moffat having dumped Madame Pompadour, whom she explains is the Doctor's daughter, and really is the daughter of the old Doctor Peter Davison. Allons-y indeed.

7. BOW TIES ARE COOL

Matt Smith gets all timey-wimey and proves he can play up front… Amy dresses as a policewoman, Rory becomes an Auton… and we collect monster cards in a plastic Tardis.

M att Smith nails the role of the Doctor quicker than any other actor. He makes his debut in *The Eleventh Hour* in April 2010 and immediately seems Gallifreyan. Landing in Amy Pond's garden and demanding a series of foods, culminating in fish fingers and custard, he's eccentric and alien and waves his arms around a lot, yet still appears trustworthy and somehow pulls off the feat of seeming to be very old despite being only 27. His angular chin and floppy fringe are very different to Tennant's conventional good looks, but they suit Smith's charismatic Doctor.

The other revelation is Karen Gillan as Amy Pond. Initially the young Amelia is played very effectively by Caitlin Blackwood. The Doctor promises to return in five minutes but returns in twelve years. It's a pleasing throwback to William Hartnell's Doctor and his inability to effectively guide the Tardis. When he does return, the blundering Doctor finds Amy dressed as a policewoman because she's working as a strippagram. Looking at her improbably long legs I'm reminded of the sexist times when Leila in animal skins was added to *Doctor Who* as "something for the dads." And now I'm in the same age group as those dads...

Gillan is excellent in the role, feisty and all red hair and Scottish rolling 'r's. Amy's very angry with the Doctor for taking 12 years to return, at one point trapping him by the tie in a car door. Her boyfriend Rory, played by Arthur Darvill, looks promising too as a Mickey-style ordinary and initially cowardly bloke suddenly confronting alien monsters.

Prisoner Zero is a little underwhelming, being an eel-like creature that can shape shift into human form and then stands around while the Doctor sorts him out, with no obvious means of killing people. But under new showrunner Steven Moffat the fears of childhood cracks in the walls are well utilised and the trio of Smith, Gillan and Darvill are instantly loved by my kids and it all looks initially promising.

As the series progresses though, I start to worry about the quality of writing. It's inevitable that the show might start to run out of ideas after four great series, but whereas Russell T Davies had subtle themes like Bad Wolf running through his first series, now the crack in time and the exploding Tardis seems too complicated and contrived, while the Doctor is becoming more and more like an American superhero, when he should be a maverick outsider.

Mark Gatiss' *Victory of the Daleks* starts promisingly and echoes the old cunning Daleks pretending to be servants in the Patrick Troughton-era story *The Power of The Daleks*. Matt Smith shines, the robotic Professor Bracewell with human memories is affecting and the world war two Daleks look impressive. But then the whole thing is ruined by the sudden appearance of a new race of what can only be described as Teletubby Daleks. The colours — red, blue, yellow, white, orange, are far too garish and the giant Daleks have large bumps at the back, They're either pregnant or have become extremely overweight after consuming too many cans of Dalek Cola while hanging with their mates waiting for the chance of universal domination.

The *Radio Times* features the new Daleks on its cover and the emailed comments are massively against the new abominations: "Like a plastic toy... pepperpots as designed by Ikea... crass merchandising ploy... giant toy Daleks... meant to be Engines of War not bloody iPods!... were they designed by Fisher Price?... WHY?... an embarrassment... don't mess with a classic design... utter rubbish... just stupid!" Very soon YouTube has videos of the new Daleks accompanied by the Teletubbies theme. Apart from that, the Whovians quite like them.

The Time of Angels/Flesh and Stone dilutes much of the menace of *Blink* and turns the Weeping Angels into much more mundane monsters - though the religious army of clerics is a good idea and Lola is very excited by the return of River Song ("her hair is so cool!") and she still says "Hello Sweetie" a lot at family meals.

I'm excited by the return of the Silurians in *The Hungry Earth/Cold Blood* and the Silurian with a Scottish accent (played by Neve Mackintosh) reminds me of the bizarre American-accented Silurian in the Pertwee era *Doctor Who and the Silurians* (the only story to ever feature the words Doctor Who in its title). Though again they're not as scary as the originals. I have much reassuring to do at the end, as Rory is consumed by the crack in time and completely erased from time and Amy's memory. My daughters' distress is ameliorated slightly as I say that I'm sure Steven Moffat will find a way of bring him back. In many ways Amy and Rory have been the best double act companions since Barbara and Ian.

Nell is now nine and is avidly enjoying the free gifts in *Doctor Who Adventures*. At dinner she dons her Weeping Angels mask and stands in front of us with her arms in the air edging closer as we try not to blink. The Matt Smith mask is a hit too, as she walks around talking about timey-wimey things.

Despite the erratic writing, the series has its good points. It's hard not to feel tearful at the end of *Vincent and the Doctor*, as Richard Curtis has Vincent Van Gogh travelling into the future to se that his pictures are finally understood and prized; while Gillan gets to do some serious acting as she ages in *Amy's Choice*.

We also get to see the Doctor play football in *The Lodger* — a scene Smith, as a former Leicester City and Nottingham Forest junior footballer will have enjoyed. The only previous example of the Doctor embracing sport was when Peter Davison landed on Earth and bowled an over in a cricket match in *Black Orchid* (the first spin Doctor?) in 1984. Now, turning out for Craig's pub side the

Kings Arms, the lads assume the Doctor is just another laddish nickname. He soon earns respect on the pitch though, as he bamboozles The Rising Sun and scores eight goals in a dramatic 8-0 win. Wonder if he could do a job up front for West Ham?

The series' finale of *The Pandorica Opens/The Big Bang* typifies Moffat's new approach. "Can you tell me what that was about?" asks Bob when we're playing for my pub quiz side the following Monday. I'm not sure either.

Matt Smith is as excellent as ever, playing the Doctor as an eccentric scientific genius unable to see the obvious. But the Doctor is too important, he's at the centre of everything, he is the most dangerous force in the universe, which causes all his foes (including more Teletubby Daleks) to unite to imprison him forever. And judging by far-left and far-right splinter parties, would an alliance between evil monsters really work? Imagine the steering committee meetings... would you delete your minutes or exterminate them?

Oh, and the Tardis exploding destroys the entire universe and means nothing has ever existed, I think. Rory comes back from non-existence as an Auton and shoots Amy with his handgun, but somehow manages to become human as the Nestenes took a memory print. Dressed as a Roman Centurion he also manages to guard Amy in the Pandorica for 2000 years, where she comes back from the dead too thanks to the Pandorica's healing properties.

Preposterously, the Pandorica, the most secure

prison in the universe, is opened by Rory using the Doctor's sonic screwdriver at the start of *The Big Bang,* which just seems a giant get out of jail card for the writer. The Doctor jumps time with alarming frequency, leaving messages for Amy, River Song does the same for him going back to the oldest cliffs in the universe, and he meets himself dying in the future mainly to show how clever Moffat is at plot twists. And then there's another escape switch as the Doctor (having had his earlier self exterminated) flies the Pandorica into the heat of the sun, which is the exploding Tardis, and therefore reboots the universe. Though he's meant to go into non-existence himself doing this, but somehow lives because Amy remembers him. Got that?

Though the Doctor arriving at Amy and Rory's wedding at the end inspires tears from the girls and causes me to shout out joyously, "Look, the Doctor's dad dancing!"

Or am I just getting old? "Steven Moffat's writing for children Dad, we understand everything," says Lola, adding, "or nearly everything." We are living in different times, where people have box sets of dvds and watch everything again and again and expect interlocking themes and complicated plots. Moffat has said he wants to return *Doctor Who* to being a series for children and play up the fantasy, fairytale elements. It's not meant to be for 50-year-olds, I guess.

It certainly has many memorable scenes and lots of action and appears to leave my children satisfied, if a little puzzled. Filming at the real Stonehenge is impressive and River Song is pretty cool and a good feminist role model. It has some good lines, like the fact they're anomalies in a dying universe, the last lights to go out. But it still feels too comic strip and superheroish. The Doctor shouldn't be the most important thing in the universe, he's a British creation and therefore self-effacing and a maverick. And the plot holes make no sense, a sort of total unravelling of logic. Too much vortex manipulation if you ask me.

Meanwhile Nell has started to collect *Doctor Who* Monster Invasion cards. They come with a free plastic Tardis with six storage drawers, for Doctors, companions, monsters, weapons, adventures and duplicates. It's a shame the front of cards feature the Teletubby Daleks, but the ratings and pictures on the back are addictive. The monsters come with ratings for scariness, cunning, strength, ruthlessness and power while companions are classified by bravery, intelligence, speed, loyalty and skill. Poor old Winston Churchill only gets 200 for speed (the same as Craig Owens) but 700 for skill.

The ratings are open to long debates and we query whether Matt Smith deserves 800 for bravery while William Hartnell only gets 600 – a bit unfair as he was a grandfather taking on Daleks with a stick! Christopher Eccleston is the bravest Doctor on 850 and Peter Davison the speediest on 700. Tom Baker tops the intelligence rankings on 850. I'm pleased to see Nell filing them and categorising them with the zeal of a collector. Wonder where she gets it from?

Two weeks before the start of season seven I hear on Radio 4's *Today* that Elisabeth Sladen has died from cancer. A big shock. I tell the girls, who have become big fans of *The Sarah Jane Adventures*, over breakfast and I think back to her signing at the Who Shop. She looked so young and had kept her illness concealed. We'll miss you, Sarah Jane.

Season 7 begins in April 2011 with a tribute to Elisabeth Sladen at the start. The new series immediately generates controversy over its scariness. The Silence are pretty eerie creatures, looking like Edvard Munch's painting of The Scream crossed with *The Men In Black*. Worse, you forget them as soon as you see them, meaning Amy has to draw crosses on her body to remind her of their appearance.

The first two-parter of *The Impossible Astronaut/Day of the Moon* sums up the way the show is going under Steven Moffat. Shot on location in Utah in the United States, it's visually stunning with Matt Smith in a Stetson and the Doctor (who is 200 years older than when Amy Rory and River last met him) being shot by an Apollo Astronaut on the shore of Lake Silenca, followed by a Valhalla-style funeral on a burning boat at sunset. "Don't worry, girls there will be a plot twist!" I reassure my family, though I'm actually quite worried that having created Teletubby Daleks Moffat might well really kill the Doctor. But then an earlier version of the Doctor turns up, 200 years younger again, to turn up in a typically Moffatian trick.

Then there's the mysterious Canton Everett Delaware III, President Nixon, the Silence menacing Amy in the loo, a scary, deserted orphanage, Amy becoming pregnant, and the Moon landings to contend with. What's it all about? Silence will fall when the question is asked.

Doctor Who is still creating news. After this epic two-parter of memorable images and unresolved questions I'm asked to contribute to a debate in the *Guardian* on whether *Doctor Who* is now too scary for children. A bit of terror at foaming seaweed rushing in through air vents never did me any harm as a kid, though I do admit to some tremors in our household:

"The Silence – who erase your memories of seeing them – were a classic Who creation and my 12-year-old daughter now has symbols on her arm to remember if she's seen them (three so far). The series has become increasingly reliant on the internal fears of children. The crack in the bedroom wall that is really a tear in space and time and the Weeping Angels that send you into the past when you blink. Clever writing, but not great for getting the kids to sleep."

Pleasingly I manage to use my 500 words to get in a dig at the Teletubby Daleks and then state that:

"There's been too much doctorin' of the Tardis by Steven Moffat and his writers... The Doctor should be a maverick wanderer, a rebel with a Tardis console, not a superhero. Now every plot seems to centre round the Doctor or his companions as being crucial to the very fabric of the universe. At the end of the David Tennant era the stars went out and the Earth moved, while in the last series we had the Tardis exploding and destroying the

universe, at least until some more infuriatingly complex time hopping by Matt Smith... At present the writers seem intent on proving how clever they are through too much complexity and too many cheap shocks."

And sounding a little like John Major going on about warm beer and old maids cycling to church, I use the pages of the *Guardian* to make a plea for traditional (or at least Ecclestonian/Daviesian) Whovian values:

"There's too much sex, too. The Doctor should be a father figure, but now every assistant seems to fall in love with him and on Saturday he was snogging River Song. My 10-year-old daughter had to turn away during this section with a cry of "Eerrgh! Yuk!" Sometimes you just yearn for aliens invading a Home Counties quarry, and a simple good versus evil plot – and with proper Daleks, not the redesigned Teletubby versions. The Christopher Eccleston story The Doctor Dances had it right: scary gas mask monsters but at the end the nanogenes repair the dead, and the Doctor exclaims: "Just this once, everybody lives!"

As the *Who* writer Mark Campbell says, being a Whovian is like supporting a football team and we all have really strong opinions on how they should play. Yet we're all still avidly watching each week, whatever our criticisms. Series 6 has a number of good stories. *The Doctor's Wife* is a title that has Lola excited as it might possibly confirm that River Song is married to the Doctor — though actually it is about the Tardis taking human form as Idris, played by Suranne Jones in suitably eccentric style. Neil Gaiman's story proves how innovative the show can still be. *The Girl Who Waited* features some serious acting from Karen Gillan, as Amy ages 36 years in an alien quarantine hospital and Rory has to choose between her older and younger versions. While *The Rebel Flesh/The Almost People* is a much more traditional story of a monastery under siege and bringing up ethical dilemmas over creating 'gangers' as cheap labour. *Let's Kill Hitler* is a jumbled mess though.

The series also has the customary revelations: Amy and her child are kidnapped by a sinister eye patch lady, Madam Kovarian, who is something to do with the Silence, I think, and we learn that River Song is actually Melody Pond, the daughter of Amy and Rory. Though I've never quite figured out why her timestream is running in the opposite direction to everyone else's, beyond it being a good plot device. The final episode *The Wedding of River Song*, again has too much going on and another reboot button pressed by Moffat. The Doctor didn't actually die in *The Impossible Astronaut*, because he was inside a Teselecta, a robot piloted by miniaturised people that had taken his form. It was the Teselecta that was shot and presumably survived the Viking funeral. There's also another aborted timeline and the Doctor marries River Song, though they then have to split up as their timestreams can't coincide (which beats a conscious uncoupling). I'm still trying to make sense of it all today.

However, the story does contain a lovely tribute to the passing of Nicholas Courtney, aka Brigadier Lethbridge-Stewart. The Doctor takes a call from Kate Lethbridge-Stewart who says that the Brigadier has died peacefully, and Matt Smith's Doctor looks genuinely affected. My football pal Michael McManus, the Brig's biographer, is deeply affected too, having becoming friends with Nick and spent many a time drinking with him in Crouch End. A good chap that Lethbridge-Stewart — let's hope they can lay on a jeep and a pint for him, wherever he might be (possibly in Cromer?).

The show shows some signs of getting back to basics when series 7 starts in the autumn of 2012. The Teletubby Daleks have been carted off to some toddler's playpen and the metallic and now slightly mad creatures return to form in *Asylum of the Daleks*, the series opener. We're also introduced to Jenna Louise Coleman, Matt Smith's new companion, months before we expected. Only she's making soufflés and in a poignant denouement is actually Oswin Oswald, a personality trapped inside a Dalek. *Dinosaurs on a Spaceship* and *A Town Called Mercy* (taking the Doctor back to the Wild West territory of *The Gunslingers*) both work well as stand alone stories not trying to fit into massive narrative arcs. The final episode of the first batch, *The Angels Take Manhattan* sees my daughters sobbing on the sofa as Amy and Rory are both sent back to 1938.

Lola recovers soon though, as to my immense pride, she manages to queue up for returns at the Almeida Theatre, and gets in to see Matt Smith in

American Psycho. Even better, a tall women gets in her way as she's about to sit down, and then she realises it's Karen Gillan. Her friend is reduced to tears by such proximity to Whovian greatness and they manage to get Gillan's autograph after the show. Even Matt Smith playing a blood-drenched murderer doesn't seem to worry them after that.

With both my daughters now at secondary school, a steady stream of teenagers enters our house asking to borrow Lola's dad's dvds. Whereas once I tried to hide my *Doctor Who* collection from prospective dates and then my wife, now my children's friends and even their dads peruse my dvds and regard me as almost cool.

There's the Christmas special of *The Snowmen* to come and then we're into 2013, which promises to be a very special year in Whovian annals. Was it really nearly 50 years ago when a boy sat down to watch *An Unearthly Child*? We shouldn't put way childish things — they're much better displayed on the dvd rack.

8. THE YEAR OF THE DOCTOR

*Peter Capaldi arrives... Judoon and Cybermen are in
the aisles at the Doctor Who Prom... The Web of Fear is
coming home... and a host of cos-playing Whovians at
the fiftieth anniversary bash.*

octor Who is 50 in 2013. That's half a
century for the Doctor and me. I first
watched the show as a four-year old in
1963 and will be 54 by the time of the anniversary
special. All sorts of treats are promised for the year,
with Steven Moffat writing a special and a big
celebration planned at the Excel Centre in London.

Season Seven Part Two is screened from March
30 and to my mind it's something of a
disappointment. Though after four brilliant seasons
of Eccleston and Tennant followed by several high
points with Matt Smith and some good stuff in Part
One of Series 7, it's perhaps inevitable that the
quality control might suffer.

The Bells of Saint Joan and *The Rings of Akhaten*
never quite get going and my daughters find Clara
"so annoying" and too passive compared to Amy
Pond. "She just hangs around the Doctor,"
complains Nell. There's much excitement about the
return of an Ice Warrior in *Cold War*, but the next
day at a West Ham match I'm sitting next to
Michael McManus and he's saying that it was just a
rip-off of *Alien* and that it's very unlikely rogue

scientist Professor Grizenko would have been allowed on a USSR nuclear submarine.

We Whovians are a critical lot, though, and in its favour it is a simple sub under siege story and there's a nasty sense of claustrophobia. The idea of the creature climbing out of its Ice Warrior suit is clever; although was it a taboo that shouldn't have been broken and did it diminish the mystique of the creatures? It's good to know the Martians care about their daughters though. The Field Marshall's face as revealed at the end is nasty enough to warrant several pauses on my TV, although again is it too much information? Is it scarier just to imagine the creature under the suit?

Journey to the Centre of the Tardis makes the whole story about Clara and her various lives again. Following on from the huge focus on Amy and her secret child it seems to me that too much emphasis is being put on the companions in the Moffat era. *Hide* isn't bad and nor is *The Crimson Horror*, though again we have too much concentration on the amusing, but over-camp figures of Madame Vastra and Strax. They are endearing once or twice, but an over-reliance on comedy strikes me as going back to the worst days of John Nathan Turner and the 1980s. *Nightmare in Silver* with its chess-playing Cybermen and the human upgrades that draw too heavily on the Borg from *Star Trek*, plus child actors and Clara issuing unconvincing battle orders, is a real dud.

The final episode *The Name of the Doctor* is more like it though. The dream conference with all the Doc's old mates including Vastra, Jenny, Strax,

Clara and River Song isn't that bad, even if the Doctor's name is something I wish Steven Moffat would stop harking on about. We don't want to know it, OK?

There's some brilliant acting from Matt Smith though, when he unexpectedly bursts into tears at the mention of Trenzalore. Richard E Grant is as good a villain as you might expect and Moffat's plot of visiting the Doctor's grave, which is in fact in the Tardis getting bigger on the outside, lends it a suitably epic feel. And then there's a glimpse of John Hurt at the end, which is tantalising. The screen flashes up: "Introducing John Hurt as the Doctor." Just what did he do to make him unworthy of the name of Doctor?

"I'm sure he isn't really the Doctor," I tell the children, "he'll be like the Next Doctor."

I suspect it might be a Moffat ruse, but Hurt is a great actor, and I've always thought he'd make a great Doctor.

In July the kids and myself go to the Royal Albert Hall for the *Doctor Who* Prom on a Sunday morning. We purchase a Tardis-shaped programme and take our comfy red padded seats. The grand old venue feels like one giant sofa inside. We find lots of small boys in bow ties — or is that just how classical music buffs dress?

The Prom begins with a lot of ethereal wailing from Elin Manahan Thomas and Allan Clayton performing *Vale Decum*, while a screen above the stage shows recordings of Matt Smith being generally epic and then all the Doctors regenerating. It's all rather moving as many a Murray Gold piece is played.

Suddenly a Judoon is coming out of the aisle next to us. Plus Vampires, Silents, Silurians and then to a big cheer, the Cybermen and Sontarans.

"That Cyberman's face fell off, look he's holding it on!" laughs a delighted Lola. Oh well, skin work is always difficult for the jobbing actor.

Conductor Ben Foster appears to have a glowing sonic screwdriver-like device on the end of his baton.

Peter Davison comes on stage to a big cheer and quips "What amazing memories you all have especially as most of you weren't even born. In some cases your parents weren't even born." He explains that he's the fifth Doctor in the classic series and, "according to my daughter grandfather to Doctors numbers 15 and 16."

Then Carole Anne Ford emerges. "It's Susan!" I tell my children. "I was the Doctor's first onscreen companion!" she says to a round of applause. She recounts her first meeting with the Daleks alongside "the great William Hartnell" and having to talk to not very terrifying Daleks minus their top halves with the actors' heads sticking out of them. "The cast were asked not to use them as dodgem cars," she adds.

Davison and Ford introduce a classic medley of *Who* tunes. It starts with men messing about with ancient tape loops and synthesisers, all filmed by a giant old wheeled TV camera. A projector shows footage of Ron Grainer in his Radiophonic Workshop. The music begins with that sinister hum whenever the Daleks appear, Susan squealing and a

Dalek issuing instructions. It segues into the classic theme of the Cybermen emerging from their tomb. It's hugely effective played on kettle drums. And now it's the synthesised squawking of the Sea Devils and their string vests, music from *City of Death* with footage of Lalla Ward and Tom Baker in Paris, Tom regenerating. Now it's excerpts from *The Five Doctors*, veering into *The Curse of Fenric* soundtrack and Ace discovering she's just met her mum. Phew.

Even the comedy Sontaran and Silurian work well. Madam Vastra and Strax emerge to a big welcome as Strax warns, "Madam we appear to be surrounded there are thousands of puny humans!" Then he mistakes the cellos for weapons and offers to guide us through the Sonta–ha! Battle song. The pair introduce Murray Gold's *Companions Suite.*

We even get some classical music — *Habanera* from *Bizet's Carmen Suite No. 2* (from Asylum of the Daleks) and Debussy's *The Girl with the Flaxen Hair* (used in *The Robots of Death*). "I told you *Doctor Who* was educational!" I tell the girls.

Daleks emerge on stage. "Attention! This Royal Albert Hall is now under Dalek control!" There's some nice Dalek comedy with conductor Ben Foster and his baton. "What is that strange thing you are carrying? Do not point it at me move away! Alert! Alert! Alert! Over acing detected! You will obey! Conductor you will remain at the platform and stop overacting this is our bit!" One of those big red Tellytubby Daleks announces that it doesn't like music about the Predator. And then a bit of Skaro pantomime: "I can not hear you! Say exterminate!

You would all make very good Daleks... Now Ben Foster, actor of the year, begin!"

"Hello!" declares Matt Smith, bouncing on stage, newly shorn, obviously enjoying himself and accompanied by Jenna Coleman. The show ends with Matt teasing us about *The Name of the Doctor* finale "What's it all about? You'll have to wait until November!" and Jenna Coleman introducing "one of the most iconic theme tunes in the universe... enjoy!"

All the monsters return to the aisles, an Ice Warrior and Silurians emerge from the alien structure in the centre of the stalls as Murray Gold's version romps along. The *Doctor Who* theme sounds tremendous played by a full orchestra. It ends with tumultuous cheers and Smith, Coleman, Davison and Ford, Strax and Madam Vastra linking arms with conductor Ben Foster and the players and taking a communal bow.

My Facebook entry that day records: "Total Whovian meltdown moment. Just seen the *Doctor Who* Prom at RAH with Matt Smith, Jenna Louise Coleman, Peter Davison and Carole Ann Ford live on stage. We were close to a Judoon in the aisles and Lola saw a Cyberman's mask fall off (he will be deleted). Der der der der der der..."

We book tickets for the Excel 50th Anniversary Shows in November and receive regular update from Crowdsurge about who is attending and how to book tickets for the various speakers.

In August the announcement of the new Doctor is given the full *Strictly Come Dancing* treatment by the BBC. On Sunday night Zoe Ball presents a special half-hour programme *Doctor Who Live: The Next Doctor*. I watch with Lola and Nell at home on our sofa. Across the room stands my trusty giant Thomson TV, purchased in 2001, on which I used to watch UK Gold repeats of *Doctor Who* back in the days when it seemed the show would never return. It appears to be as indestructible as the Doctor, though really we should get a flatscreen soon.

The Sunday papers all think Peter Capaldi is favourite for the role, though other actors are mentioned such as Olivia Coleman as a female Doctor, Dominic Cooper, Stephen Mangan, Tom Hiddleston, Rory Kinnear and Daniel Kaluuya and David Harewood, either of whom would be the first black Doctor.

Regenerations used to just happen. The Doctor felt a bit queasy at the end of one series and the new man arrived at the start of the next. Now there's a studio audience of Whovians with a Tardis and Dalek on display. Pundits are brought out from the green room to talk to Zoe Ball. Peter Davison says the role never leaves you and tells Zoe about the difficulty of making a speech at daughter Georgia Moffett's wedding to David Tennant. We have opinions from Lisa Tarbuck, that kid from *Outnumbered* and Donna's grandfather, Bernard Cribbins, who reveals he once had discussions about playing the Doctor. Professors Brian Cox and Steven Hawking even get to put up an opinion, as do Katy Manning, Bonnie Langford, Janet Fielding and Anneke Wills.

After much preamble Zoe produces a sealed

envelope and announces: "Please welcome the 12th a Doctor, a hero for a whole new generation. It's Peter Capaldi!" He emerges on stage amid red and yellow beams of light and a cloud of smoke looking slightly bashful and waving. The theme tune beats out.

"Daddy, will he be a good Doctor?" asks 12-year-old Nell.

"Girls, he's older than me! He'll be brilliant, though he might swear a lot," I answer. "It's OK, he'd been in *Local Hero*. Denis Lawson cooked Danny's rabbit. And he was a Roman merchant in *The Fires of Pompeii*. Hey, I'm younger than the Doctor again!"

"It could be you next, Dad," suggests Nell.

"What a good idea!"

Ball interviews Capaldi for the next five minutes and it emerges Peter's a fan since childhood. He received the call in Prague when his agent said "Hello Doctor!" and he knew the role was his.

Seemingly every paper runs a 'swearing Doctor' spoof in the style of *The Thick of It* in the next few days. The *Guardian* asks if he will be saying "Fuckity-bye Daleks!", while a spoof internet video has Capaldi calling Daleks "hordes of fucking robots" and replying to Clara's "run you clever boy" with "fuck off!"

Meanwhile plans are being made to exploit my children for a feature in the *Guardian's* Family section. The *Doctor Who* Prom makes me realise just what an influence *Doctor Who* has been on my family life and that my whole parenting philosophy has been based on never minding SATs or key stage four results, but concentrating on the really important thing about being a father — instilling in my children a love of Whovian values.

The *Guardian* sends round photographer David Levene and they say they want Whovian props. So I remove our inflatable Dalek from the cellar, which is covered in so many cobwebs it looks like it should be in *Asylum of the Daleks*, and try to pump it up with a bicycle pump.

It takes ages to find a suitable nozzle after visiting several bicycle shops. "It's not for a football or even a bike, it's for an inflatable Dalek," I finally confess to a cycle man in Stoke Newington. "For my kids, obviously." He looks dubious but eventually suggests a yellow nozzle that just about does it. It takes several hours of pumping in the extension with the neighbours probably assuming I have a collection of inflatable women in there. It has separate pouches to inflate for the arms and gun and eyepiece. The Dalek is prone to more deflation than even George Osborne can provide and I have to guard against a wilting eyestalk. But a quick pump before the snapper arrives and it's as solid as it will ever be.

David assembles us in the kitchen as Nicola makes her excuses and leaves us to it. The inflatable Dalek is propped up on a kitchen table as I hold Nell's Tardis box of *Doctor Who* cards. Nell wears her Weeping Angels mask from *Doctor Who Adventures* and Lola wears the Cyberman head we found at a car boot sale. The picture looks great when the article is published in October. I might not have cracked it writing comment on the serious political issues of the day, but I have managed to get my kids wearing *Doctor Who* masks into the *Guardian*. And for once all the comments emailed in by the readers are nice. Especially Resource13507 who writes, "wish my dad had been like that."

Meanwhile we decide to watch the anniversary special show at home rather than in the cinema. The sofa seems the right place to be. The showing clashes with a rearranged West Ham game against Chelsea at 5.15pm and for a foolish moment I suggest going to the game and leaving early to watch the Doctor and catching up with any early bits I miss by recording it. My two obsessions are colliding. Nicola says "You really must watch it with her, she'll be upset if you don't." Lola says we have to watch it live because it's a special moment and she has to watch it with Nell and me. Football is not registered in her vocabulary bank. I feel a bit like Davros in *Genesis of the Daleks*. I have created the ultimate Whovian. And she's right. She'll be in therapy for years if I miss the start. There will be other football matches, but only one 50th anniversary special. I agree to forgo using my season ticket and devote the whole weekend to *Who*. What was I doing?

Three days after my piece is in the *Guardian* the BBC announces that several missing episodes from the Hartnell/Troughton eras have been discovered in Nigeria. It's superb timing for the anniversary. The *Daily Mirror* erroneously claims that every missing episode has been discovered but that's too good to believe.

Christian the Webmaster pens a Facebook parody of *Football's Coming Home* called "Who is coming home..." ending with the line "and Victoria screaming!"

A search of Twitter suggests some likely finds, with Michael the Whovian and several others suggesting it's *The Web of Fear* and *The Enemy of The World* and possibly *Marco Polo*.

We have to wait several days for a BBC press conference, which announce that, incredibly, nine episodes have been found. We now have the complete *The Web of Fear* minus episode three (episode one was already in the archive) while all of *The Enemy of the World* has been recovered. The rumours on Twitter were right. I'm up at midnight to download the episodes from iTunes. And despite needing my sleep it's impossible to resist playing them.

It's amazing how well *The Web of Fear* stands the test of time and warehouse space. My childhood re-emerges from dark tunnels. The story has brilliant Underground sets, a sense of constant claustrophobia, Yetis with web guns (no one knows why they have web guns but it just seems right), bodies covered in cobwebs, creeping fungus... and fine performances from Troughton's Doctor, Frazer Hines' kilted Jamie and Deborah Watling's screaming Victoria. The Yetis look decidedly cuddly in the above ground battle of Covent Garden, but the stunt work is advanced for its time and the subterranean stuff is still scary today.

It's a fine debut from Nicholas Courtney as the Brigadier (then just Colonel Lethbridge-Stewart) and he produces a lovely bit of acting when he returns exhausted to the Underground HQ and simply mutters "Gone…" after his men have been utterly wiped out by the Yetis. The characters are a delight too, including a dodgy journalist, a sixties redbrick university-educated woman scientist and a very non-PC cowardly Welsh soldier (what did 1960s BBC have against the Welsh?). It deserves its status as a classic. My daughters watch too and humour me by saying it's not bad for the olden days of *Doctor Who*, when unbelievably no one had mobile phones. Lola even loads it onto her iPod, spanning five generations of changing Whovian technology.

The next day we stand on the tube platform glancing nervously down those circular tunnels. The found episodes make the front page of the *Mirror* with a large picture of Patrick Troughton, Frazer Hines and Deborah Watling and the headline "THE LOST DOCTOR Revealed: the nine missing *Who* episodes found after 50 years."

The Enemy of the World is surprisingly enjoyable too. It begins with a hovercraft chase in Australia (ok, it's really a beach in Littlehampton, West Sussex) and is interesting for featuring no monsters as *Doctor Who* goes a bit *James Bond* and Jamie throws some punches. Patrick Troughton plays two characters and gets to adopt an outrageous foreign accent as the Doctor's doppelganger, the evil dictator Salamander. It all ends with a memorable scene of Salamander being sucked out of the Tardis doors and into the time vortex.

The two Troughton stories top the iTunes

download chart, seeing off both *Homeland* and *Breaking Bad*.

The *Day of the Doctor* on November 23 edges closer. Even I start to think the BBC might be overdoing it a little bit. In the run-up there's *The Science of Doctor Who* with Brian Cox and *Doctor Who: The Ultimate Guide* in two two-hourly episodes on BBC3, going through the eras of all the Doctors with contributions from companions and writers. Lola and Nell find a spin-off prequel *Night of the Doctor* featuring Paul McGann and the Sisterhood of Karn on iPlayer. McGann looks great in the role and you realise what a fine Doctor he could have been.

Peter Davison directs an affectionate spoof on the whole 'who's in the anniversary show?' hysteria in *The Three Doctors Rebooted*. It comes complete with Sylvester McCoy mentioning that he's in *the Hobbit*, a cameo from Georgia Moffett and David Tennant and John Barrowman being exposed as having a wife and children.

There's a two-page feature in the *Daily Telegraph* on another lovely bonus for Whovians, *An Adventure in Time and Space*, a dramatized version of the creation of *Doctor Who* written by Mark Gattis. David Bradley plays William Hartnell beautifully, with just the right mix of insecurity and cantankerousness, while the drama gets over just how big a chance the BBC's Sydney Newman took putting the show in the hands of BBC establishment outsiders Verity Lambert, a rare woman producer, and Warris Hussein an Egyptian-born director. It's worth watching just for the shot of a Cyberman in facial stocking taking a tea break during *The Tenth Planet*. We see Hartnell drinking whisky at home and being irascible with his granddaughter, before slowly starting to enjoy being a hero to millions of children. His reluctance to leave the show as his health declines is ultimately very moving. Hartnell hands over to Pat Troughton and there's a nice shot of Matt Smith acknowledging his legacy at the end.

Even Google has a special Doctors logo around its search engine. The *Guardian's Weekend* magazine has a cover feature "Who's that girl?" interviewing female companions from every era, including Billie Piper, Katy Manning, Louise Jameson, Sophie Aldred and Freema Agyeman among others. *Time Out* has a two-page feature on "Deconstructing the Doctor" and the *Observer* runs a feature on the top ten *Doctor Who* stories of all time, controversially excluding such classics as *The Web of Fear*, *Genesis of the Daleks*, *Blink* and *The Girl in the Fireplace*. It's hard not to recall the wilderness years and all those commissioning editors who said, "it's not for us" whenever a feature on *Doctor Who* fans and their extraordinary steadfastness was suggested.

And then *The Day of the Doctor* arrives. There's a nervous feeling in my stomach I normally only get on Cup Final days. On Facebook I post: "Is there some sort of *Doctor Who* event today? I've not heard much about it…" While one of my Facebook friends controversially posts that "I hate to remind you but *Doctor Who* is a show for children". As if…

That morning's *Guardian* has a two-page feature

on the anniversary. Mark speculates on what monsters will be in the special and speaking to Moffat about the weight of history on his shoulder and also an unrepentant Michael Grade (boo!), the man who killed the Doctor in 1989, who says that he won't be watching it because he hates science fiction. While Zoe Williams is at the Excel for the 50th anniversary celebrations and "the fancy dress party that never ends." She interviews various fans about their Sylvester McCoy jumpers and there's a large photo of fan Adam Bentley in a costume combining facets of most of the Doctors, including a Tom Baker scarf.

Finally the evening arrives. We sit down in front of the tele with a ready supply of crisps and the promise of dinner after the 75-minute special. From the moment we see Mat smith hanging from the Tardis over Trafalgar Square it all seems to go very quickly.

"That's my Doctor! I feel quite emotional..." says Lola as David Tennant appears, snogging Queen Elizabeth I (or is it a Zygon?). John Hurt is superb as the weary War Doctor and there's some great humour as this grumpy old Time Lord full of gravitas criticises Tennant's sand-shoes and Matt Smith for not being able to say anything without moving his arms around and of course using phrases like "timey-wimey." And none of them think to try pushing open their unlocked cell door in the Tower of London, unlike Clara, so intent are they on sonic screwdrivering it over four centuries of calculations.

The battle scenes with the Daleks on Gallifrey look suitably epic and Billie Piper acts really well as the conscience of the Time Lord's Doomsday weapon, which appears to be clockwork. It's good to see the Zygons again, if they are used mainly for comedy, while the steely Kate Lethbridge-Stewart wanting to blow up all of London is a nice nod to her dad the Brigadier.

And there's a real sense of a Dostoyevskyian moral crisis as the Three Doctors return to the burning Gallifrey – is it better to fail doing the right thing or succeed doing the wrong thing? And how many children died on Gallifrey? Amid a lot of technospeak, Gallifrey is saved by the three Doctors concealing it in a picture on Earth by using the stasis cube, as you do. When the curator's voice is heard at the end, I want to say, "It's Tom Baker!" but stop myself because I'm thinking, no it can't be. But it is.

"It's Tom Baker!" shouts Lola.

"I never expected that... Would you like a jelly baby?" I mutter. "So Gallifrey's been saved... he's not the last of the Time Lords, apart from Susan, Romana, the Meddling Monk and the Master... everybody lives!"

We've been left with two massive revelations. Gallifrey survives and there's another Doctor – is he Doctor 8.5? I'm pleased and relieved that Gallifrey lives – albeit in stasis in a Time Lord painting — as it always felt presumptuous of Russell T Davies to have destroyed the whole race. And it's poignant that the War Doctor won't remember that he did the right thing and nor will his successors. And for all my worries about overcomplicated timestreams, I'm left admiring the imagination and sheer verve of

Steven Moffat.

And then we switch over to the after-show party on BBC2. Zoe Ball is hosting again with Rick Edwards and there's a room full of companions sitting around tables being served blue drinks by Ood barmonsters. It's a bit like Jools Holland's Hootenanny on New Year's Eve rewritten for Whovians. Zoe goes round the largest ever gathering of companions. Carole Anne Ford is "exhausted" after watching it, while Ian Chesterton is "astonished" and Bernard Cribbins loved it.

Matt Smith arrives in a black polo-neck and is served fish fingers and custard as he reveals that it really was him hanging from a crane above Trafalgar square. John Hurt with his grey goatee exudes charm and says it was fantastic working with "the boys", as he terms Matt and David. There's a lovely video of Tom Baker being esoteric and declaring "Am I in it? I had a fling with a girl who was a curator at the British Museum once."

Peter Davison, Sylvester McCoy and Colin Baker give their verdicts. Zoe and Rick talk to Whovians in Australia and selected Whovians in the studio, while there's a shambolic live satellite link up with One Direction in Los Angeles. But it's all very celebratory and a good way to end the night as I sip a pint of Bishop's Finger in honour of Tom Baker. But that's only the start of our Whovian weekend.

The next day we're up early and off to the Excel Centre for the 50th anniversary bash which starts at ten o'clock. I'm going with Lola and her friend Yasmin. Sadly, Nell's performing in her Christmas ice skating show at the Sobell Centre on the same Sunday. She's been having lessons all year and rehearsing for the big show. Nicola is going along to watch her, but she's very upset to be missing the Who-fest. I feel terrible. "Brave heart, Nellsy," I tell her, "next year I'll make it up to you."

In that morning's *Observer* there's a full-page review of the special is "more of a Whatian than a Whovian", but she and her family enjoyed it and it was all worth it for the line "I may be a weak and feeble woman but then so did the Zygon."

We negotiate the Overground and the Docklands Light Railway. You belong to us. You shall be like us. There's a man from America wearing a cool bow-tie on the DLR train as we approach Prince Regent station. People are coming from all over the cosmos to pay homage to the Doctor.

It's one of those occasions when psychic paper would be very convenient. I'm carrying a wad of A4 print-out tickets the size of a small book, three for our initial entry and then three each for every talk going by various *Who* luminaries. At this stage it feels safe to put on my Tom Baker scarf. We're given shiny neck passes with a *Doctor Who* logo confirming our Whovian status. We are in the Ice Warriors group.

Inside the Excel it resembles one of those giant space freighters where Cybermen are always secretly stored in the cargo section. We pose for pictures across a giant backdrop of all 11 Doctors at the end of the hall. Within the main atrium Whovians mingle around the food stalls. Hey, that's the real Lalla Ward walking past...

"Look Dad, Dalek dresses!"

"And there's a Patrick Troughton!"

"Fezzes are cool!'

And we spot Tardis dresses too. Plus Dalek bumps, several Peter Davison Doctors with celery in their lapels, more bow ties and tweed jackets than you can shake a sonic screwdriver at. There's even a chap dressed as the Next Doctor, David Morrissey's Doctor who wasn't, which is a nice piece of cos-playing. We find a cafe on the balcony and order Americano and tea and look at the strange races mingling below. We are not alone. *Who* is all around.

We enter the main hall for the SFX show. There's a Cyberman on stage and Danny Hargreaves, the show's special effects guru is showing daunted young Whovians in bow ties how to fire a blaster at the Cyberman and cause a proper SFX cyber death. He gets out his wind machine and creates a wall of flames at the front of the stage. Questions are invited from the audience and it emerges there's fans here from Australia.

Next we rush up the escalators to the Classic Lounge 11.20 event. Matt Smith is rumoured to be in one of the rooms but we stick to our designated audience with Wendy Padbury, Maureen O'Brien and Peter Purves.

I last saw Wendy Padbury in the Who Shop, but here she is again in her black leather jacket, laughing at the footage of her character Zoe draped across the Tardis console, a moment of sexual frisson for many adolescent boys now running TV companies. "I couldn't even spell astrophysicist!"

Padbury says she is now an agent. Padders, as my friend Michael the Whovian calls her, has some interesting tales of the projected kinky and sexist Troughton-era story that was set in a women's prison planet but ultimately cut – though laddish Fraser Hines was of course in favour.

Maureen O'Brien giggles hysterically as she is shown her overacting fleeing from Frankenstein's monster in *The Chase*. She hasn't seen it since 1965, which is a nice moment and proves that actors take the show a little less reverentially than Whovians. She's great, admitting that she had no interest in *Doctor Who* after appearing as a companion and couldn't understand the fuss, but had now came back to it.

Compere Toby Hadoke describes Peter Purves as a legend from not one but two classic TV series, *Doctor Who* and *Blue Peter*. Toby shows footage of Purves as a hillbilly encountering a Dalek at the top of the Empire State building and then a bearded Peter in *The Daleks' Master Plan*, clad in a double breasted sixties corduroy jacket and getting very animated as Katerina is swept to her death from an airlock.

Steven Taylor was an extremely underrated companion and Purves gave a very convincing performance as an astronaut who had been imprisoned by the Mechanoids for two years in *The Chase*. He has plenty of tales of William Hartnell's mix of charm and irascibility. Peter's voice is strangely authoritative and comforting to a man raised on *Blue Peter* sofas, Patch the dog and papier-mâché models of the Moon.

Surprisingly Lola and Yasmin seem genuinely interested in these tales of old actors from the 1960s.

When the session is over we head to the food area for some astronomically-priced curry. In the Gents I find myself standing at the urinal, flanked by two junior Whovians in tweed jackets and bow ties. Weird.

The main exhibition area is reached through the doors of the Totter's Lane Scrapyard, scene of the very first episode in 1963. Fans queue to have their pictures taken at this iconic site. Inside it's pretty much Whovian nirvana. All the Doctors' costumes are displayed on mannequins, there's real Daleks, K9, a giant BBC shop, and stalls for Big Finish audio, the Forbidden Planet and lots of t-shirt companies. A live Cyberman is having his bottom pinched by a female fan. On Stage 2 Caitlin Blackwood, the actress who plays young Amy Pond is being interviewed. There's a practical demonstration of cyber-marching for kids with a BBC choreographer.

We buy some Dalek socks and the Van Gogh exploding Tardis picture for Nell at the £5 shop and a River Song sonic screwdriver for Lola at Forbidden Planet. By the Big Finish stall we bump into my pal Michael McManus, author of the Brigadier's autobiography *Still Getting Away With It*. We discuss West Ham's loss to Chelsea in a desperate bid to prove we are well-rounded people and OMG that's Sophie Aldred over there...

Our party walks into a wardrobe trailer full of clothes from the series. It's smaller on the inside with racks of clothes on every edge. That's John Simm's shirt... Lola and Yasmin get very excited by Amy Pond's blouses.

At 2pm it's the Regenerations show in the main hall, with Sylvester McCoy, Colin Baker and Peter Davison. Sylvester McCoy does a lot of clowning with his brolly, trying to get into the onstage Tardis, sitting on the edge of the sofa, falling off the back and lying across his companions. "Did you know he's in *The Hobbit*? They're doing a movie for every page," quips Baker, repeating the self-deprecating joke from Davison's lovely spin-off the *Three Doctors Re-booted*. The three share an easy intimacy on stage, and there's a nice description from McCoy of how the fans gave the show "mouth to mouth resuscitation".

Straight from that show it's up to the Classic Lounge for an audience with Bonnie Langford, Mark Strickson and Lalla Ward. Mercifully Bonnie isn't wearing anything shiny and her voice is deeper and much less irritating in 2013. Mark Strickson mow lives in New Zealand where he produces natural history films, while Lalla Ward sews artistic cushions and is, of course, married to Richard Dawkins.

Ward has aged well and is of some interest to us as she's distant relation of Nicola's. I recognise something of the 'not-we' attitude of my wife as Ward tells Toby Hadoke that she didn't watch the 50th anniversary show last night and she isn't going to watch it. But Ward softens with a little gentle questioning from Hadoke and just as she's becoming more expansive the girls insist we rush off to see Matt Smith in The Eleventh Hour session.

And indeed there is Matt in his crew-neck jumper and jeans, Jenna Coleman in grey fluffy jumper with n animal on the front, "showruuner" Steven Moffat and *Day of the Doctor* director Nick Hurran. There can't be many events where the compere picks out "the lady on the front row dressed as a Dalek" to ask a question.

The giant screen above the stage shows the audience a clip of Tom Baker in the previous night's *Day of the Doctor* and Matt Smith says how much he enjoyed playing in it. Though signing his cheques as the Doctor still hasn't paid off, he adds. Nick Hurran talks of the magic of having David Tennant back in that suit again and Smith says of the Zygons meeting Time Lords plot, "it's all as mad as a box of lunatic frogs".

Steven Moffat is proud of the way the show has cracked America and says no-one has a negative word to say about Matt, His comment, "The way Matt carried himself as the Doctor is something of which the Doctor would be proud," sparks a round of applause.

And there are fine words from Moffat on what makes the Doctor so special: "Heroes tell us who we want to be... this hero they didn't give him a gun, they gave a screwdriver to fix things... there will never come a time we don't need a hero like the Doctor."

Phew. Another session to go too. At 4.50 it's another session in the Classic lounge with that great actor Julian Glover, aka Scaroth Last of the Jagaroth. Sadly no-one asks him how he and the

Countess Scarlioni performed in the bedroom – was *everything* wrapped up in a human skin mask? He does talk about Douglas Adams' script and being a Bond villain though. We also have the giant Michael Kilgarrif, the former Cyber leader from *Tomb of the Cyberman* and Stephen Thorne, voice of such monsters as Sutekh, Eldrad and Omega. We're shown a clip from *The Daemons* where Azal can't understand Jo's willingness to sacrifice herself for the Doctor and Toby Hadoke remarks: "Azal must have been the first *Doctor Who* monster to be confused to death."

Then we gatecrash another session in an adjacent room and find Anthony Reid, the script editor of the *Invasion of Time*, talking about the budgetary and logistic problems of the production and how the Tardis interior was filmed in a hospital basement (check).

Then it's back to the main exhibition hall for Whovian meandering. My pal Christian was here the day before and found himself in the regulated queues thinking that maybe the show has got too popular, that he remembers the days of interviewing stars with just a 30 diehard fans in a room. And for a second I find myself thinking likewise. Where were all these fans during the wilderness years? Are the New Whovians just glory-hunters? Where were they when being a *Doctor Who* fan meant you were one notebook up from trainspotters and never got to have a partner?

But then can you be a Whovian without wanting to attain universal domination? Do we really want to be purist fans of a dying art form, destroyed in the Time War by Michael Grade and destined never to return? Would I deprive my children of the joys of Eccleston, Tennant and Smith? Isn't it a force for good that so many people are Whovians now? Have I the right... And sod this, there's Sophie Aldred over there...

We find Sophie Aldred signing audio cds and I take her picture with Lola. That's Sophie Aldred with my daughter... I'm a proud man. And Lola spots Hugo from *Les Miserables*, so she's doubly happy.

At the Forbidden Planet shop I find myself in the queue with Michael McManus, telling him that the David Tennant sonic screwdriver I'm buying is for Nell not myself, honest.

Sadly the time comes to leave. As we stand in the atrium Lola talks to a French woman in full Lalla Ward schoolgirl outfit, looking ready to participate in *City of Death*. How did that happen? It's been a lovely day, immersed in the regeneration game and all the useless but wonderful ephemera of the Whovian universe. There's a wave of overpowering affection for this British institution that is 50-years-old and still in front of the sofa. So it's quite right that we've come out on the balcony to wave a tentacle or two. Happy birthday Doctor – all of you.

9. ON THE WHOVIAN SOFA

*The Doctor lands in Loughton... finally getting to use a
sonic screwdriver on the Whovian chatshow circuit.*

Host a Whovian event and they will come.
It's March 2014 and an astonishing 70 or so
Doctor Who fans have congregated at
Loughton Library in Essex. The Essex Book
Festival — with whom I've previously worked
promoting my book *The Joy of Essex* – have seen
my article on being a Whovian in the *Guardian* and
have asked me to interview Mark Campbell, author
of *Doctor Who: The Complete Guide.* On the
promotional flyer I'm billed as "a lifelong
Whovian" which, somewhat sadly, makes me feel
rather excited. Finally I've made it as a *Doctor Who*
pundit.

It's proving to be another year of epic Whovian
meetings. After a West Ham game my pal Michael
has taken me to the Club for Acts and Actors where
Richard 'Captain Yates' Franklin, the last surviving
member of UNIT, is standing at the bar. I've also
been interviewed by Richard Wilson about my book
on Essex for his forthcoming series *A Drive With
Richard Wilson.* Sitting on a bench in Harlow I'm
able to congratulate him on his role in *The Empty
Child/The Doctor Dances* and to prove what a nice
man he is he later posts my daughters signed
pictures of himself as Gaius in *Merlin*.

On the day of the Loughton Library event Mark

Campbell meets me in his car outside Loughton tube station. We drive to the library and as we walk in we're accosted by a Whovian male who asks where he can sell a complete set of signed Christopher Eccleston dvds and a few years' worth of *Doctor Who Adventures* with free gifts. We suggest the Who Shop as a starting point.

Mark and myself sit in the green room (OK, it's an office) with coffee and biscuits, trying to work out the intricacies of microphones that look like they should be attached to Davros. We sneak a peak through the door at the audience and it's frankly astonishing. I'd expected ten people, but there's a whole room of punters who have paid £5 each. They range from children to teenagers to middle-aged men, and there a surprising number of women. Clearly Clive's wife's look of astonishment when she discovers that Rose is interested in Clive's Internet theories about the Doctor would no longer happen.

It's great to see so many different t-shirts. One reads "Time Traveller from Gallifrey", while others credit Daleks, Rose and the Tardis and there's even a young woman in a renegade *Star Trek* one (we'll forgive her that as I like it too). Nicola is in the audience with Lola and Nell and I feel rather proud.

Julia from the library gives a short introduction and we emerge from our room to applause. We are miked up and seated in two comfy chairs. It almost feels like being on *Parkinson.*

Luckily I've raided Nell's bedroom for her sonic screwdriver to use as a prop. I beep the sonic at the audience and announce that they're 90 per cent human, apart from some Zygon shapeshifters at the back and the odd Krillitane. The Sonic might also be useful in the event of a fire alarm, although as we know from the 50th Special, it doesn't work on wood.

My first question is about Essex connections with *Doctor Who*. Mark is able to mention *The Lodger* being set in Colchester but filmed at Cardiff, and one of his favourites, Jon Pertwee's *Carnival of Monsters*, being filmed on Tillingham Marshes.

Then it's on to *The Day of the Doctor* which he thinks was great, even if *The Name of the Doctor* looked like it was thrown together and was a big disappointment.

Campbell's *Doctor Who: The Complete Guide* is not as authoritative as *Doctor Who: the Television Companion,* by David J Howe and Stephen James Walker, but at 35,000 words it was never meant to be. It's a dip-in book with cast and filming details and a brief summary of both classic and new *Doctor Who* up to Series 7.

The Complete Guide was first published in 2000 and Campbell wanted to shake up accepted wisdom and make some controversial judgments. He's not afraid to debunk some accepted fan classics. We discuss his low scores for some stories ("I was generous with one out of ten for *Let's Kill Hitler*!") and the fact that *The Dæmons* only got six out of ten and *Genesis of the Daleks* scored eight out of ten ("it was great but too long.")

Mark talks of the suspension of disbelief that is required for classic *Doctor Who*: "Everyone forgets that in one of my favourite stories, *The Caves of Androzani*, there's a really crap monster that's a bloke in a rubber suit, but we overlook it because in *Doctor Who* it's the scripts that count."

Campbell has been a fan "since forever" and grew up with Jon Pertwee and his tale of fascination and then obsession is endearingly familiar to most of us present. "If you're like me you'll watch the dvd, first just the story, then with the commentary, and then with the production subtitles," he explains.

Mark recounts taping Pertwee episodes with a cassette recorder and then "crossing over to the dark side" after collecting the 1970s Weetabix models of characters and starting a fanzine called *Skonnos* (named after the planet featured in *The Horns of Nimon*) that he advertised through the pages of the Doctor Who Appreciation Society magazine.

Amusingly, Campbell tells us of the time his eventual wife forgot to record an episode of *The Curse of Fenric*. "I put the phone down on her. That's a bit sad, but I thought I'd never see it again. I've forgiven her now."

We also learn that Campbell did a Power Point presentation and projected images of *Doctor Who* on to the side of his house on that monumental day in March 2005 when the Doctor returned after 16 years. He had a pair of mannequin legs sticking out of his wheeliebin, as you do, in honour of the scene where Micky is eaten by a Nestene-controlled bin. Not even a brief burst of sound bleeding over from Graham Norton presenting *Strictly Come Dancing* could ruin his day — "and no-one called the police either!"

Having watched every episode of *Doctor Who* ever made, Mark is now starting again and is currently up to William Hartnell's *The Romans*.

We chat about the various Doctors and when we mention the Colin Baker there's a spontaneous question from a boy in the audience, who says that surely he must like *Attack of the Cybermen* because it contains a working chameleon circuit in the Tardis and the scrapyard at 76 Totter's Lane from the very first episode. I'm impressed that someone so young has seen Colin Baker dvds and is standing up for working chameleon circuits.

Campbell replies tactfully that he prefers his police box to remain a police box and that the programme should stand alone without continuity references to *Who* mythology. Someone else asks why the BBC eventually put the kibosh on it in 1989 and Julia from the library has to ask for the questions to wait until after the interview, such is the ferment.

We discuss David Tennant and Mark says how much he loved it when Tennant made that great speech only to exclaim that it's from the *Lion King* in *The Christmas Invasion*, proving that like Tom Baker he could veer from comedy to seriousness.

I'm able to repeat my Matt Smith anecdote to the audience. The day before the event my pal Martin texted me to say he was at Islington Council Offices buying a resident's parking permit next to Matt Smith, who was presumably getting a permit for his Tardis. Though you'd have thought he could just use psychic paper instead.

Campbell thinks that Smith nailed the part

quicker than any other actor, but has become an arm-waving caricature of himself. We find common ground on the Moffat era, with Mark suggesting that all the Doctor has to do is shout "I am the Doctor!" and the aliens run off, whereas he wants the characters to be in fear of their lives.

He agrees the story arcs are too complicated: "It's very difficult to write something that's simple. Anyone can drop things into a story and not explain it. Steven Moffat says 'what's wrong with being complicated?' but to me that's not good writing. *Blink* was complicated but it all made sense within that story. Today *Doctor Who* is visually stunning but the script is almost the last thing they think about. With Russell T Davies the script came first."

Though as Mark Campbell admits in his book, supporting *Doctor Who* is rather like supporting a football team, where we'll criticise the tactics and results and claim things were always better in the past, yet staunchly evangelise about the programme to all outsiders.

After a brief foray into the rediscovery of *The Web of Fear* and *The Enemy of the World* and what episodes Mark would like to find (possibly *The Savages*), we move on to audience questions.

Silence does not fall when the question is asked. Feeling like David Dimbleby on *Question Time* I get to say, "the gentleman in the back row next!" We have questions about the Paul McGann prequel *Night of the Doctor*, which Mark thinks proves McGann was the best Doctor we never had, and then a question about *Doctor In Distress*, the naff 1985 Live Aid style single featuring Colin Baker singing that is "possibly the worst single I've ever heard."

A boy asks for his views on *Spearhead From Space* and shop window dummies coming alive, as his father laughs, "Dad indoctrination!" Another audience member comes in with a nice anecdote saying that when he was six none of his class would go to the shops the Monday after *Spearhead From Space* was broadcast, as "no-one wanted to walk past Hepworths!" Controversially Campbell says he prefers *Terror of the Autons*.

Still the questions come. There's one on the guilty pleasures of liking non-classic episodes like *The Underwater Menace* and *The Web Planet* (with lines lovingly quoted by the audience member), something on *An Adventure in Space in Time*, and a request for his best cliffhanger (the asker says he actually wanted Sylvester McCoy's Doctor to fall at the end of *Dragonfire* as the cliffhanger was so bad.)

We cover the budgets question, including the toy tank in *Robot, with* Mark making the important point that throwing money at something doesn't make a good story. Someone asks about *Vincent and the Doctor* and then a woman asks about the Time War.

To my immense pride, my daughter Nell asks what his ideal Doctor would be like, if he could make up a Doctor. Mark suggests someone eccentric, like Tom Baker who's a bit weird, and also "bonkers in real life."

"Excuse me because I feel like I've sat through a lecture in nuclear physics," says a woman in the third row to much laughter, "I've never actually sat through a whole episode [gasps from the audience] but I was wondering how *Torchwood* is perceived by the fans?"

Campbell throws out to the audience and the consensus is that *Torchwood* is OK but not essential viewing, while Mark thinks it was odd it was for adults only and describes it as "*Scooby Doo* with adults."

A cross-section of Loughton Whovians can talk about the show forever. There's a discussion of the best quotes — "I'd opt for 'You're a beautiful woman, probably,' from Tom Baker," says Campbell. Then it's the possibility of a woman Doctor, what makes a good companion ("someone who's not a plot device like Clara," says Campbell) and a question on how he cut the material down for his book.

As the organisers suggest we wind up, the final question deals with going into the past and why some events are immutable and others aren't. We conclude that it's usually whatever the writer wants to get them out of a plot hole. Mark is speculating on the fact that if the eruption at Pompeii had to happen then does that mean that an alien spaceship has also crashed into Big Ben?

Wisely the organisers wind up the gig at this point and we are greeted with warm applause.

The organisers from the Essex Book Festival hand out their evaluation sheets and director Belinda Farrell remarks how pleased they are to get so many men into the library as they rarely attend events. Mark Campbell sits down to sign books and we admire the teenagers' Tardis t-shirts and discuss the upcoming series.

You couldn't really have a better demonstration of the enduring love for a British TV show. What makes a good *Doctor Who*? Is it the writing, the acting, the monsters, the direction, its Britishness or a combination of all these things? Yet we all just know that when it works there's no other programme on TV that can match it.

I'm sure we should all be using our time for more important political activities, but being a Whovian is harmless, it keeps us in the community, it's fun and useful for pub quizzes. And sometimes as Peter Davison told the Cybermen, it's the small things in life that make a difference. Resistance really is useless.

"Well done Dad," say my daughters, and maybe I've finally proved to them that I am a contender, at least in the Whovian world.

Nicola is amazed too. "I *knew* everything they were taking about and I'd seen lots of those episodes. What have you done to me?" Despite being 'not-we' (that's a reference from *Kinda*) she's understood a lot of what people were talking about through a curious process of Whovian osmosis.

It's pleasing my family are here. Other dads affect gravitas or can put up shelves. But I have a whopping great *Doctor Who* dvd collection, a Zygon coaster and a Dalek mouse mat.

I feel like I've given my children a good start to life in the universe. And when my time comes to regenerate perhaps they'll think only this of me — he was a true Whovian Dad.

ALSO BY PETE MAY

What Are Words Worth?
Man About Tarn
Goodbye to Boleyn
The Joy of Essex
There's a Hippo in my Cistern
Flying So High
Ageing Body Confused Mind
Hammers in the Heart
Rent Boy
West Ham: Irons in the Soul
Sunday Muddy Sunday
The Lad Done Bad

Printed in Great Britain
by Amazon